"This book importantly provides strategies for engaging children with autism spectrum disorder (ASD) and other disabilities in sporting activities. It offers needed, practical information for parents, coaches, teachers and others. The reader is guided to consider sport as a means to physical fitness, community engagement and quality of life. The book is an important contribution in building 'welcoming' communities, and critically addressing under-studied opportunities in sport for persons with ASD. A highly recommended read!"

— David Nicholas, Associate Professor, Faculty of Social Work, University of Calgary

"As a gymnast with Asperger syndrome, I have had to overcome many of the issues highlighted in *Getting into the Game*. I was very fortunate to start gymnastics at the age of three and so I am testament to the fact that sport can help young people with autism spectrum disorders overcome fears and difficulties in all aspects of their lives. I would highly recommend this book to parents or teachers who have children with autism. It is full of information and advice that will help readers gain a better understanding of ASD and how to introduce and teach sport to children on the spectrum."

— Philip Davis, 26, gymnast, "Special Olympics" silver medallist (Athens, 2011), former Senior and Junior British Champion (2002, 2005), and coach at the Croydon School of Gymnastics

"Written in a friendly voice that is readily accessible to both professionals and families, *Getting into the Game* offers concrete suggestions for including people with autism in sports and other physical activities. The authors clearly understand both the challenges faced by individuals with autism and the need for clear, visually supported teaching strategies that lead to success. This is a 'must-have' book for parents, teachers, and coaches who are dedicated to the eradication of 'couch potato syndrome' as a side effect of autism!"

— Dr. Pat Mirenda, Professor in the Department of Educational and Counselling Psychology and Special Education, University of British Colombia

Getting
into the
GAME

of related interest

Get out, Explore, and Have Fun!
How Families of Children with Autism or Asperger Syndrome
Can Get the Most out of Community Activities
Lisa Jo Rudy
ISBN 978 1 84905 809 4
eISBN 978 0 85700 385 0

Yoga for Children with Autism Spectrum Disorders
A Step-by-Step Guide for Parents and Caregivers
Dion E. Betts and Stacey W. Betts
Forewords by Louise Goldberg, Registered Yoga Teacher and Joshua S. Betts
ISBN 978 1 84310 817 7
eISBN 978 1 84642 498 4

Everyday Activities to Help Your Young Child
with Autism Live Life to the Full
Simple Exercises to Boost Functional Skills, Sensory
Processing, Coordination and Self-Care
Debra S. Jacobs and Dion E. Betts
Foreword by Carol A. Just
ISBN 978 1 84905 238 2
eISBN 978 0 85700 482 6

Playing, Laughing and Learning with Children on the Autism Spectrum
A Practical Resource of Play Ideas for Parents and Carers
2nd edition
Julia Moor
ISBN 978 1 84310 608 1
eISBN 978 1 84642 824 1

Speak, Move, Play and Learn with Children on the Autism Spectrum
Activities to Boost Communication Skills, Sensory Integration
and Coordination Using Simple Ideas from Speech and
Language Pathology and Occupational Therapy
Lois Jean Brady, America X. Gonzalez, Maciej Zawadzki and Corinda Presley
Illustrated by Byron Roy James
ISBN 978 1 84905 872 8
eISBN 978 0 85700 531 1

Gardening for Children with Autism Spectrum
Disorders and Special Educational Needs
Engaging with Nature to Combat Anxiety, Promote
Sensory Integration and Build Social Skills
Natasha Etherington
ISBN 978 1 84905 278 8
eISBN 978 0 85700 599 1

VERONICA SMITH AND
STEPHANIE Y. PATTERSON

Getting into the **GAME**

*Sports Programs for
Kids with Autism*

Foreword by Connie Kasari

Jessica Kingsley *Publishers*
London and Philadelphia

First published in 2012
by Jessica Kingsley Publishers
116 Pentonville Road
London N1 9JB, UK
and
400 Market Street, Suite 400
Philadelphia, PA 19106, USA

www.jkp.com

Library of Congress Cataloging in Publication Data
Smith, Veronica.
Getting into the game: sports programs for kids with ASD/Veronica Smith and Stephanie Y. Patterson.
p. cm.
Includes bibliographical references.
ISBN 978-1-84905-249-8 (alk. paper)
1. Sports for children with disabilities. 2. Physical education for children with disabilities. 3. Autistic children. I. Patterson, Stephanie Y. II. Title.
GV709.3.S56 2012
796.087--dc23
2012002413

British Library Cataloguing in Publication Data
A CIP catalogue record for this book is available from the British Library

ISBN 978 1 84905 249 8
eISBN 978 0 85700 551 9

Printed and bound in Great Britain

CONTENTS

FOREWORD BY CONNIE KASARI 9

ACKNOWLEDGMENTS 13

PREFACE 15

PART 1 ACTIVE ENGAGEMENT IN SPORT: THE BASICS ON
HOW AND WHY TO GET STARTED

CHAPTER 1   Why Participating in Sports is
Great for Individuals with ASD 19

CHAPTER 2   Choosing a Sport 28

CHAPTER 3   Working With Your Coach: Parents' Corner 39

CHAPTER 4   Supports and Strategies for Learning in Sport........ 54

CHAPTER 5   Learning Supports for Children with ASD 65

CHAPTER 6   Keeping Everyone Organized and Motivated:
Strategies for Encouraging Volunteer Engagement..... 78

PART 2 SPORTS FOR NEW ATHLETES WITH ASD: BASIC
SKILLS, STRATEGIES, AND ONGOING ADAPTED
PROGRAMS

CHAPTER 7   Bike Riding: Getting on the Road 93
Janine Halayko and Veronica Smith

CHAPTER 8   Let's Go Skating! Introducing Your Skater with ASD
to the Ice for the First Time 120
Stephanie Patterson and Vivian W. Ng

CHAPTER 9   Swimming: Life Skills for the Water 141
Laura Dumas and Veronica Smith

CHAPTER 10   Kicking the Habit: Martial Arts Training for Families
with Children with ASD 164
Jonathan Rivero and Stephanie Patterson

CHAPTER 11   Tennis: The Perfect Match.......................... 188
Shafali Spurling Jeste, Richard Spurling, and Stephanie Patterson

CHAPTER 12   Soccer: Join the Soccer Team!........................ 210
Veronica Smith

REFERENCES... 240

ABOUT THE AUTHORS 244

THE CONTRIBUTORS.................................... 245

SUBJECT INDEX 248

AUTHOR INDEX....................................... 254

FOREWORD

Finally, a book about the possibilities of sports for children with an autism spectrum disorder (ASD)! Although involvement in team and individual sports plays an important role in children's lives and well-being, children with ASD often avoid rather than engage in such activities. Such avoidance could be due to their intensive therapy schedules, the noisy, chaotic, and unpredictable nature of the sports environment, or the lack of coaches with the skill set to teach them. Thus, for families of children with ASD the possibility of adding a sport to a child's already busy life may seem more trouble than it's worth.

Getting into the Game: Sports Programs for Kids with Autism Spectrum Disorders uniquely addresses these issues for children with ASD, and convincingly argues that adding sport to a child's busy schedule can be an enhancement rather than a bother. Veronica Smith and Stephanie Patterson tell personal stories of the importance of sports in their lives, and of successful sports instruction for children with autism. Particularly noteworthy is that the book focuses on how to start playing a sport, as well as on the basic skills, strategies, and adapted programs necessary to excel in the sport. Each of the chapter authors provides a cogent account of why their sport is great for children with ASD, along with specific suggestions on how to develop basic skills and to achieve successful sports literacy.

The book is organized in two parts. Part 1 introduces basic information about sport, strategies for choosing a sport, working with coaches and volunteers, and adapting educational strategies for use in the sport environment. This part provides critical information and tools to help families make informed decisions, and gives coaches ideas to help them improve the sporting experience for children with ASD. I would venture a guess that this part may help parents or coaches with teaching *any* child who is a first-timer in a sport, or who is deciding they would rather be watching their favorite cartoon than running the bases.

Part 2 walks readers through six different sports (biking, skating, swimming, martial arts, tennis, and soccer). Readers are introduced to the benefits and potential challenges presented by each of these unique sport environments and provided with tips and strategies for successful first experiences in each sport. Basic foundational skills are presented in a step-by-step fashion for each sport, with photos and diagrams as well as charts and organizers to help families to make a plan and support the new athlete appropriately. Each chapter also highlights an existing and successful adapted community sports program for students with ASD in North America, and includes the personal story of a family that has used the program.

This book comes at a timely juncture for children with autism. The Centers for Disease Control recently announced that 1 in 88 children are now diagnosed with an autism spectrum disorder, and about 60 percent of children test without intellectual impairment (below 70 IQ; see Centers for Disease Control and Prevention, 2012). Thus, there should be many more children with ASD who are educated in general education classrooms alongside their neurotypical classmates. Playing individual and team sports will become more and more essential to the overall education of children with ASD and will offer them opportunities to increase their feelings of inclusion and belongingness in both general education and community settings.

Another reason for the timeliness of this book is the increased risk of obesity among children with autism (Curtin et al., 2010). Their tendency to play alone, or to engage in sedentary activities (such as playing video games), puts children with ASD at risk of negative health and developmental outcomes. Interventionists may unintentionally contribute to more inactive means for engaging with other children by concentrating social skills interventions on board games at school rather than more active playground games. According to recent reports, approximately a third of children with autism are overweight or at risk of being overweight, in large part due to inactivity (Curtin et al., 2010).

Beyond the obvious benefits of sport involvement to physical health and well-being, children can gain immense social benefits both with family and community peers. Sports can offer the child with ASD activities to share with siblings, and parents and children can widen their social circles by meeting other families on the team. For children with ASD, feelings of marginalization and loneliness at school increase with age (Bauminger and Kasari, 2000; Kasari et al., 2012). Younger children are less aware of feeling lonely but tend to have infrequent peer interactions at school and often do not know how to play the games in the playground (Kasari et al., 2012). One approach to helping these children to engage more with other children, and thus increase the likelihood of developing friendships, is to involve them in sports, whether at school or in the community. Children can gain physical literacy and confidence, which will provide them with the motivation to engage in activities with other children. Beginning early may stave off the intense feelings of loneliness and isolation that adolescents feel at school. Physical literacy is important to develop, whether at school or in the community, in order to increase the potential for generalizing skills and confidence across settings.

This is a book for families, clinicians, coaches, and anyone who wants to improve both children's sports literacy and ultimately their developmental outcome. Families will feel encouraged to try a sport with their child, and clinicians and coaches may find their trepidation dispel. Smith and Patterson provide excellent detailed strategies translating what we know about effective instruction in the classroom into creative uses in sport environments – for example, utilizing a moving visual schedule which uses simple language so as to not overwhelm a child who may be learning a new physical skill; or providing specific prompts to teach a skill, which creates structure and encourages and motivates children. Tips are provided to deal with such sensory related issues as the too-tight helmet, scratchy uniforms, uncomfortable shoes, and noisy gyms or rinks. Importantly, this book includes strategies for children who range in their ability to communicate, and provides supports to teach and include not only children who can use spoken language but, rather, children of all abilities.

Getting into the Game exposes much of the "hidden curriculum" in sports etiquette and behavior, providing very specific information about the language, the first steps, how to practice, and troubleshooting challenges that may be encountered. This book will be most helpful to those children and families who are yet to have a positive experience in sport, or those who may feel that they are not ready to give sports a try. Sports do not need to pose a risk to children with autism, but can instead be a means to develop "physical literacy," peer relationships, inclusion, and, above all, to have fun while doing so!

Dr. Connie Kasari
Professor, Center for Autism Research and Treatment and
the Graduate School of Education and Information Sciences,
University of California at Los Angeles

ACKNOWLEDGMENTS

PHOTOS AND FIGURES

Many people assisted us in creating and capturing the photos and illustrations used in this book. We are very thankful for their creativity and helpfulness in making the sports "come alive."

Thomas W. Arden is an aspiring artist living in Vancouver. While studying art at Langara College, he is also an avid photographer and keen BMXer. He collaborated with Erin denHartigh to create many of the illustrations in this book.

Rachel Barskey lives in Vancouver, B.C., where she recently graduated from the Faculty of Law at the University of British Columbia. Rachel's other interests include writing, oil painting, and illustration.

Erin denHartigh is a student at Emily Carr University of Art and Design. She is a talented painter and lithographer and enjoys exploring in the more remote parts of the world (currently with Thomas in tow).

Trent Magus is an Occupational Therapist living in Edmonton, Alberta. His hobbies include photography, both out of and under the water!

Harvey Rubin is a retired motion picture cameraman currently teaching tennis in Los Angeles privately and for ACEing Autism. Harvey also represents the United States Professional Tennis Association as their tournament photographer.

Ryan Yao is a sports program manager for the Canucks Autism Network. He is a talented photographer and creative soccer coach.

FAMILIES

A big thank you to the many families who shared their stories while we were researching this book. Several of them generously described their child's journey in sports. Thank you to the parents, David, Don, Susan, Chris and Julie, Mira, and Karren who contributed to the chapters and to their children, Josh, David, Daniel, Benjamin, Zoe, and Jesse and Zack, for being such good sports! Also, a big thank you to the many children and coaches who helped us out by agreeing to be photographed.

COLLEAGUES AND WELL WISHERS

We spoke to many amateur sports enthusiasts who helped us improve the accuracy of what we wrote. As well, many family members and friends provided much encouragement and support. Thank you to all.

Finally, we would like to thank Dr. Connie Kasari for writing the Foreword – we appreciate her thoughtful consideration of the contribution this book may make for individuals with ASD and their families.

PREFACE

For the authors, participation in sports is far more than an amusement of childhood, it provides the context for us to learn about how the world works and allows us to understand more about ourselves and others, giving us the confidence to take risks and participate in many new and challenging opportunities in life.

From both our personal experiences in sport and our work with families with children with autism spectrum disorder (ASD), we have been inspired by those who have benefited from participating in sports. However, for many children with ASD, participation in organized sports may constitute a risk rather than an opportunity due to the many challenges that are associated with ASD. We understand that families may be reluctant to enroll their children in sports, and some coaches or physical education teachers may feel unprepared to promote participation in sporting activities. Our hope is that through the many resources that we will draw your attention to in this book, parents, teachers, and coaches who are hesitant or unsure how to encourage students with ASD, to "get into the game" will discover new methods and become enthusiastic about including children and young adults with ASD in sporting programs.

We have divided this book into two parts: the first provides a description of the benefits of sports participation, provides some guidance about how to select a sport, and outlines coaching and learning supports to make participation in sporting activities beneficial for children with ASD. In the second part, we describe six common sporting activities that children participate in around the world including biking, skating, swimming, martial arts, tennis, and soccer. One chapter is devoted to each sport – in each, we examine the entry-level skills taught within that sport and provide examples of adaptations or supports to facilitate teaching these skills to new athletes with ASD.

We have included various forms and checklists throughout the book, which are indicated by the ✓ symbol and available to download from: www.jkp.com/book/9781849052498/resources

We've had to limit our discussion to six sports but we know that there are many more activities that children could choose from. Our hope is that you will be able to apply some of the ideas and strategies to the sports we describe and to other sports that you may explore as you encourage or support your new athletes with ASD to "get into the game"!

PART 1

ACTIVE ENGAGEMENT IN SPORT

The Basics on How and Why to Get Started

Chapter 1

WHY PARTICIPATING IN SPORTS IS GREAT FOR INDIVIDUALS WITH ASD

What you will learn in this chapter
- The many benefits of participating in physical activities.
- What is understood about activity levels for individuals with ASD.
- Several parent-reported benefits of sport participation for children with ASD.

To begin, we think that it is important to briefly examine the research and anecdotal reports that support the health and lifestyle benefits of sports participation, especially for people with ASD. While much of what we cover in this chapter may seem like common sense, there might be a few gems of information that will convince you (whether you are a parent, a person with ASD, a teacher, or a coach) that participation in sports and other physical activities is beneficial.

BENEFITS OF PARTICIPATING IN PHYSICAL ACTIVITY AND SPORTS FOR KIDS OF ANY AGE

Across the lifespan there are many paybacks from participation in physical activity and sports. The most obvious benefit is physical: increased levels of cardiovascular fitness, higher levels of muscle endurance, decreased body fat, improved co-ordination, and a slowing of the impact of chronic disease (US Department of Health, 2008). For younger athletes, there is an accumulation of research demonstrating that regular physical exercise influences cognitive development and learning at school (Sibley and Etnier, 2003; Tomporowski, 1986). Just as important, participation in sport and recreation has many known mental health and social benefits. It provides a context for some people to form friendships and to observe growth in their skills and competencies that make them feel good about themselves. For others, it provides meaning and purpose in life (Law *et al.*, 2007). There really are very few negatives about getting exercise. We all know from our personal experiences that we feel better after we've had a bit of exercise and (if we don't overdo it) it's usually a lot of fun too.

Below, you'll find a summary of five key research findings about the benefits of sport participation.

1. You will live longer

Countless studies have confirmed the link between regular physical activity and good health and longevity (e.g. Haskell *et al.*, 2007; Lee and Paffenbarger, 2000; Trost *et al.*, 2002). The key to these positive benefits, however, is the word "regular." The benefits are realized when the activities are frequent enough to make a difference. For example, significant health benefits can be obtained from just 30 minutes per day of moderate (e.g. swift walking) activity. This level of activity reduces the risk of premature mortality in general, and a raft of other significant health concerns like coronary heart disease, hypertension, and diabetes. It also improves mental health and is important for bone, muscle, and joint development (US Department of Health and Human Services, 2002).

According to the US Department of Health and Human Services (2002), all children are recommended to accumulate 60 minutes or more of moderate to vigorous physical activity per day. However, it is estimated that approximately half of children are considered inactive and do not accumulate this recommended amount in any one day. Sadly, this is not just an American problem. We found reports from Canada, Australia, the United Kingdom, and New Zealand that echoed these findings – kids in most developed countries aren't getting the recommended level of physical activity per day. This phenomenon has become a health concern in most Western countries. Most children, teens, and adults need to get more physical activity to reap the health benefits. Figuring out how to make physical activity a "regular" part of your daily routines, especially for people with ASD, is one of the reasons we wrote this book.

2. You will develop "physical literacy"

By acquiring fundamental movement skills (e.g. running, jumping, throwing) and fundamental sport skills (e.g. hitting a ball with a bat, throwing a ball in a hoop, jumping over a bar) children and teens are able to enjoy a variety of activities, which leads to lifelong participation in sport and physical activity. This knowledge has recently been dubbed "physical literacy" by the Canadian Sport for Life Organization. According to Canadian Sport for Life

(2011), "individuals are physically literate when they have acquired the skills and confidence to enjoy a variety of sports and physical activities." Just like literacies associated with reading and math, physical literacy is essential to getting along in the world.

Physical literacy develops as a result of being physical in a context that supports learning. In childhood, team and individual sport participation provide a context for this learning to take place. Sport instruction places demands on participants to listen to verbal instructions, observe the actions of others, process information quickly, and respond to cues – all within a social context. In some cases physical literacy also involves understanding how to compete or perform well. Physical literacy is acquired through participation in a variety of physical activities where children learn to read what goes on around them, understand their own physical response, and react accordingly.

Without "physical literacy" there is a tendency for children to drop out of sports or opt out of physical activities altogether. Poorly developed physical skill is one of the main reasons that children choose not to participate in motor activities. By engaging in physical activity early and by investing many hours in physical play or sport, children are more likely to develop physical literacy. Participating early in life sets up a positive cycle of events – children develop fundamental movement skills, they experience more enjoyment moving their bodies, and develop more positive beliefs about themselves and physical activity. With this positive outlook there is a lack of perceived barriers to engaging in physical activity and, consequently, children become more confident in their own ability to engage in regular physical activity.

3. You will learn better

There is a growing body of research indicating that time spent participating in sports and physical activity will have collateral benefits in the classroom (Sibley and Etnier, 2003; Tomporowski, 1986). The academic benefits associated with sports participation have been described in a number of ways: better grades, improved academic skills, better attention in class, and more positive attitudes to school. Without getting into a detailed physiological explanation, when we are physically active, certain neurochemicals associated with learning and brain growth are stimulated. As well, regular exercise increases blood flow to the cortex, which enhances oxygenation resulting in better brain functioning. These factors highlight the importance of ensuring that children get sufficient activity to optimize their cognitive functioning, which contributes to improved learning at school and other educational settings.

4. You will stay active longer

Being physically active early in life is strongly associated with being active later in life (Burtton and Martens, 1986; Skard and Vaglum, 1989; Weiss and Ferrer-Caja, 2002). Researchers have found that teens who do not learn the fundamental movements associated with sports tend to engage in few physical activities as adults. Active adults, on the other hand, report regular sports participation as children and feel more confident in foundational physical skills of balance, agility, and strength. So, learning foundational sport skills early makes a difference for a lifetime. Research has also demonstrated that when children and teens withdraw from physical activity early (as early as 10 or 12 years old) they turn to more inactive and/or unhealthy choices during their leisure time. As well, the development of a variety of motor skills and sports is related to a greater likelihood of a lifetime of leisure activity (e.g. Kohl and Hobbs, 1998). The message here is clear – in order to live a life that includes physical activity throughout, you need to start early and mix it up a bit!

5. You will have more fun

Probably the most obvious benefit of participating in sports and physical activities is that it is fun – or at least it should be an enjoyable experience for parents and children. Too often, in some children's leagues and lessons, the pressures to be the *best* take precedence over the "fun" aspect. Parents, kids, and coaches need to keep in mind that *fun* should be the most important reward of participating. We need to remember that when we're playing any game or sport, there are new opportunities to meet new friends, learn new skills, and participate in the community. All of these factors add up to a greater sense of well-being and a more positive quality of life.

It is clear that the benefits of physical activity and sport are universal for all children (and adults) – including those with developmental diagnoses, such as ASD. Let's look at what we understand about the patterns of activity in sport and physical activities for teens with ASD. As you'll soon see, there is reason for concern.

PATTERNS OF ACTIVITY FOR KIDS AND TEENS WITH ASD

Pan and Frey (2006) examined the physical activity patterns in children and adolescents with ASD. Their findings were not positive. They found that kids with ASD were less active than children in the general population – and you will recall from our discussion above that general physical activity levels are low for most children, so this is a big concern. Similar to the general population, children with ASD were more active than adolescents with ASD, but neither children nor adolescents on the spectrum engaged in long bouts of exercise. The lack of participation seems to be due to a number of factors: the environments that children grow up in, their own unique preferences, and some constraints that are imposed by lack of information and supports. We provide a sketch of these issues below.

Are children engaging in physical activity at school?

The answer to this is yes and no. Rosser and Frey (2005) observed that children with ASD had high physical activity levels during recess time at schools and they speculated that this was because the children used the playground equipment or engaged in activities that were unstructured or did not require much social interaction with others. However, recess represents a small portion of a child's day and, for many children with ASD, is often curtailed when teachers remove children early to ease transitions back to the classroom. As well, during scheduled gym or physical activity times, participation for children with ASD was not always for the same length or as skill focused. Children with ASD were often supervised by one-to-one aides, and educational goals were more often focused on participation goals rather than physical education skill goals.

Do children with ASD engage in extracurricular activities?

Children with ASD participate in far fewer afterschool or extracurricular programs than children in the general population. Pan and Frey (2006) found that lack of extracurricular participation was particularly pronounced in adolescents, where only 10 percent reported spending time in physical activities outside of school. One issue, according to parents and teachers, was the availability of physical programs for children and teens with ASD. When programs were available, parents noted that supports were inadequate and lead to frustration or lower levels of enjoyment or participation. Adequate supports encompass many issues – staff or coach training in understanding autism, sport-specific activity modification, and resources to engage volunteers or assistants to assist with modifications. When not addressed, these issues make participation in organized physical activities unappealing or too potentially risky for parents to consider for their children with ASD.

Do kids with ASD like sports?

The answer to this is not so simple. Pan and Frey (2006) asked the children and teens whether they liked sports and, if not, why not. Some of those with ASD reported that they did not like activities that made them feel sweaty and others reported that they simply did not like group activities, especially team sports, but might feel more enthusiastic about individual sports such as swimming or taekwondo (or other martial arts). Although most individual sports occur in a group context, they were more appealing for kids with ASD because there were no performance expectations that could influence the group outcomes, which made these sports less stressful.

WHAT ARE THE IMPLICATIONS FOR KIDS WITH ASD?

What this means is that some children with ASD may be participating in sports when they are young but they are not participating enough and, for several reasons, this participation wanes as they get older. One can speculate on why this is so. Reports from parents indicate that the lack of participation is probably due to a number of factors. After diagnosis, some families choose to spend a lot of time in early intervention and say that it is too challenging to add sport activities to an already jam-packed schedule. Other families find that they have attempted to include their children in extracurricular sports activities but the program staff or coaches have inadequate training or not enough supports to teach their children effectively. Consequently, the children learn few foundational skills, develop inadequate "physical literacy," and become unmotivated to continue in that activity – or any other activity that involves balance, co-ordination, agility, or speed. Other families complain that for them there are no suitable programs available in their communities or, when coaches are willing to include their children with ASD, they confess to feeling unprepared to teach them. So, there is a multitude of reasons and all of it adds up to a cause for concern for individuals with ASD.

In adulthood many individuals with ASD, if not employed, may have more time on their hands. If they have limited recreation skills, their participation in community activities and their opportunities to interact with peers with and without ASD will be greatly restricted. Extra free time coupled with limited recreation skills often lead to a sedentary lifestyle that, in turn, can lead to health and social problems (Schleien, Ray, and Green, 1997).

In short, we concur with Pan and Frey (2006) who suggest that children with ASD are at risk for health problems associated with inactivity. What is needed are efforts to ensure that children with ASD have the opportunities and supports to develop "physical literacy" just like their peers – in order to make this happen, they need appropriate physical activity options that meet their unique needs.

BENEFITS OF SPORTS FOR KIDS WITH ASD

Despite the grim picture painted above, we interviewed many parents and coaches while collecting information for this book and we became firm believers: participation in sports is great for kids with ASD! Not only is it great for the kids but there are countless benefits for the families (parents and siblings alike) that participate alongside them. Additionally, we learned that it is also beneficial to the coaches and volunteers who make it happen. Below we summarize what we learned.

- *Children with ASD can learn new sport-related skills.* We learned that finding a good sport program and quality coaching helped many young people with ASD acquire sports skills across a range of activities. They also developed critical lifetime leisure skills that included an appreciation for continued participation in recreational pursuits.

- *Children and families feel part of their community.* Overwhelmingly, we learned that families of kids with ASD who found an appropriate recreational activity for their child felt part of a broader community that was inclusive and supportive on many levels.

- *Therapy goals of communication, socialization, and independence are realized on the field (or in the pool, on the skating rink, in the tennis court, etc.).* Families described "breakthroughs" in goals that had been worked on in therapy across several domains – but especially communication, socialization, and independence. From simple activities of listening to a coach, making eye contact, choosing a partner for a drill – the children progressed in areas that would extend to other areas of their life. We were struck with how many happy faces we saw on the soccer field and tennis courts – these new skills were being learned in an atmosphere of fun and playfulness – a delight to see!

- *Opportunities for independence are expanded.* Learning how to move your body in a new environment leads to all kinds of opportunities for independence – exactly what parents want for their children. New understanding of your own body's physical abilities to balance, co-ordinate a new move, or speed up or slow down is the ultimate act of independence. Learning new sports skills is replete with these opportunities.

- *More people in your community know about ASD.* What was really fascinating about the fabulous coaches that we interviewed was how well known they were by the autism community and the community at large. By being an example of how to include individuals with ASD they had done a lot to make ASD more visible and understandable to the whole community. Also, by getting out and participating, more children with ASD demonstrate that they can be athletes despite some unique learning needs which expands how the community perceives ASD and provides new hope for future athletes with ASD.

SUMMING UP

The research reviewed in this chapter confirms that physical activity is beneficial for all children and adults alike, including those with a diagnosis of ASD. Physical activities experienced through vigorous play as well as organized community sport and recreational activities have a positive effect on many aspects of child development ranging from individual learning to community attitudes toward athletes with ASD. Research indicates that the earlier children become "physically literate" the more likely they are to remain physically active for the rest of their lives. There is a worrisome trend that all children and especially children with ASD are engaging in less physical activity than is recommended to live healthy lives. Given the benefits of sports participation, there needs to be a greater push to encourage and support children with ASD to "get into the game" in order to develop the physical literacy that will allow them to have lifelong engagement in community sports and recreation. In the following chapters, we do our best to summarize what we have learned about how to set up programs, how to design strategies to support, and how to break down the fundamental skills sports to accommodate new athletes with ASD who require additional considerations to participate.

We're excited to share all that we've learned about successfully supporting athletes with ASD in the sport environment. We hope you'll join us for the ride!

RESOURCES

Organizations that support physical activities for kids, teens, and adults

Australian Sports Commission
www.ausport.gov.au

National Health Service (UK)
www.nhs.uk/livewell/fitness/Pages/Fitnesshome.aspx

ParticipAction Canada
www.participaction.com/en-us/Home.aspx

President's Council on Fitness, Sports, and Nutrition (USA)
www.fitness.gov

Sport and Recreation New Zealand
www.sparc.org.nz

Chapter 2

CHOOSING A SPORT

What you will learn in this chapter
- New ways to think about concerns that make a family hesitant to enroll their child with ASD in sports programs.
- Things to consider when choosing a new sport for your child.

Some families are reluctant to involve their children in sporting activities. In this chapter, we will: (1) address fears and concerns that might prevent a family from enrolling their child with ASD in sports, and (2) then explore some questions to help guide the selection of the sport that is ideal for your child and family.

HESITANT TO ENROLL YOUR CHILD IN SPORTS? READ ON

As noted in Chapter 1, research investigating the activity patterns of children with ASD indicate that many of these children are not participating in a sufficient level of physical activity to encourage healthy development. Parents have several very real concerns that make them hesitant to enroll their children with ASD in sport. Let's consider some of these concerns below.

1. He's too sensitive

Many adults with ASD report being particularly sensitive to certain sounds, sights, textures, and smells (e.g. Grandin, 1995). These sensitivities appear to be related to sensory processing problems. Many studies have found that children with ASD have more sensory processing issues than other children. These issues can present in a number of ways. For example, an individual with ASD may be:

- *Distressed by certain sounds.* Evidenced by: hands over ears, moves away from the sound, cries.

- *Sensitive to touch.* Evidenced by: stiffens or moves away when touched, takes off shoes or clothes, rolls sleeves up or down.

- *Excited or distracted by visual patterns.* Evidenced by: focuses intensely on the pattern on a soccer ball, pattern on a tennis racket, or markings on the ice.

- *Resistant to new foods or experiences.* Evidenced by: refuses certain textures or smells.

SENSORY STORIES

Sometimes children are so distracted by sensations that they need help to remember to stay focused or figure out ways to self-calm. One interesting intervention developed by a group of occupational therapists is the Sensory Story (Marr *et al.*, 2007). The idea with these stories is that they help to develop a child's insight into their sensory issues and remind them to follow the strategies that are useful to self-calm. Here is a sensory story developed for a child who attends swimming lessons in an indoor pool.

Jason's swimming lesson story

Children go to swimming lessons to learn to swim and be safe around the water. Sometimes in the pool, the children gather around the swimming instructor to learn about what they need to do to learn to swim.

When the children are in the pool, the instructor might tell them something new, show them how to do something, or help them to do something.

The instructor wants the children to be quiet and stay still in the pool. The teacher does not want children to move around and be loud.

Sometimes being still and being quiet is hard to do.

There are special things I can do to make it easier to be quiet and listen. I can get my swimming noodle and hang on to it while I am listening. Hugging the swimming noodle helps me to get calm.

During group time, I can put my feet flat on the ground. I like to push my feet down and feel the pool floor. This helps me to stay quiet.

If I have trouble sitting still, I can take a deep breath to help me listen and learn.

When group time is over, I stretch my arms up high and take a deep breath. Now it is time to practice and I know what to do. Being quiet and still in my swimming lesson helps me learn!

In sporting venues, athletes need to adjust to many new sensory experiences. The swimming pool, the skating rink, the soccer field, the tennis court, or the martial arts studio (dojang) each present the participant with a unique constellation of sounds, smells, and visual experiences. Some participants approach these experiences with excitement and curiosity, but overly sensitive children may struggle to adjust to these new environments. The sensitivities may be so distressing for some students that it is difficult for them to benefit from the instruction within the sport lesson. For some students, these sensitivities may lead to inappropriate behaviours that make it challenging for them to learn and that may be disruptive or distracting for others.

Interventions have been developed to target some of these sensory issues. While no one intervention is the magic bullet, some are effective in increasing children's participation in leisure, play, and social activities. In Table 2.1 below we provide descriptions of some of these interventions and describe how they can be adapted to sporting environments. Reflecting on these suggestions and adapting them to suit other circumstances may be useful for children who experience sensory issues that prevent them from participating in sport.

2. He only likes one thing

Some children with ASD have certain enthusiasms or ways of playing that take precedence over all else. They prefer to do only the things that they are interested in and this makes it difficult to introduce new activities. These issues can present in a number of ways. For example, an individual with ASD:

- May engage in repetitive activity with or without materials (e.g. twiddling, flicking).

- May have a special interest that occupies much time and energy.

- May play in an unconventional way and have limited pretend play.

- May resist changes in familiar routines and plans.

- May pursue his or her own agenda and exclude the suggestions of others.

- Will prefer to be in control and stay in control of what happens.

Table 2.1 Environmental sensory issues

Environment	Sensory issues	Things to try
Skating rink	**"Visual noise."** Some children may find that the lights at the arena are too bright.	**Glasses to filter light.** Children who are sensitive to the light may already have glasses that help filter out or decrease the amount of light reaching their eyes. These may be worn during skating, provided that they do not hinder the child's ability to safely move around the ice surface. **Sunglasses with very light tint** may be worn to class at the discretion of the instructor
	Visual noise can also be created by the markings and piles of snow that can accumulate on the ice.	**Get out there early.** Get on the ice before it becomes cut up by the blades of other skaters and before coaches mark up the ice with pens and other materials.
	"It's too cold in here." The temperature of the rink may be a new experience.	**Dress appropriately.** Make sure that your child has warm gloves and a hat to contend with the cold. Most coaches warm the new skaters up so this ceases to be an issue in lessons.
Swimming pool	**"Lots of sounds!"** Swimming pools are noisy, especially when swimming lessons are being conducted, including mechanical noises, announcements on loud speakers, children in the water, and instructors on the deck. NOTE: **Indoor and outdoor pools** have different challenges. For example, sounds may be amplified in indoor pools while outdoor pools may have environmental noises (e.g. from a nearby road).	**Try wearing earplugs (ear band).** These can help decrease sensitivity to the noise levels. **Visit the pool before the first class,** which will not only allow the child to become familiar with the facility and activity, but may also help the child become used to the level of noise through repeated visits. **Attending lessons at a swimming facility that is not as busy** or registering for lessons during a less busy time of the day will usually offer a less noisy environment.

cont.

Table 2.1 Environmental sensory issues *cont.*

Environment	Sensory issues	Things to try
	"It smells funny in here." Many people are sensitive to the smell of the water in the swimming pool.	Social story. For some children it helps to write a social story about why swimming pools smell. Letting children know before they arrive that the pool will have a special smell and that the smell of chlorine is associated with keeping the pool clean may help ease the reaction.
The great outdoors	"Wind, rain, heat." The weather is distracting to many of us, and can be disturbing to someone who is sensitive.	Unfortunately, there isn't much that can be done about the weather! But we can: • Dress appropriately (e.g. wearing gloves is useful for children who don't like the sensation of rain on their hands) • Hats and sunglasses. The sun may prove too bright for some, and sunglasses and/or hats with visors can help decrease this distraction. • Talk about the new sensations. This may be beneficial for those children who do not have the language to describe these new sensations and experiences.
Equipment texture	"Rubber and fuzz." Some kids may become distressed when touching things that are fuzzy and rough (tennis ball) or rubbery (racquet grip/bike handles).	Gloves may be worn at the discretion of the instructor as long as they allow for a good grip on the tennis racquet or bike handles to be maintained and do not impede movement.

Introducing new activities and routines may be challenging but it can be done. For most children with ASD, expanding repertoires of play and interests is a goal within their home and school programming. Participating in a sport and recreational activity is a great place to start to work on this goal. However, you need to remember to introduce new activities slowly. Most children with ASD can ease into a new activity if they are given transition cues and visual schedules that help to clarify changes and what is coming up next. In Chapter 4, we will introduce how some of these strategies can be used to introduce sport activities.

3. He's not that co-ordinated

Motor problems are reported in many children and adults with ASD but they are not universal. Some children with ASD have been found to have motor impairments such as poor co-ordination and motor planning (Hilton, 2011) and others have been found to have motor skills that are in line with developmental age (Stone *et al.*, 1999). Children with motor development issues:

- May have dexterity and co-ordination problems (making running and moving quickly a challenge).

- May demonstrate poor eye–hand, eye–foot co-ordination (this can make ball handling skills challenging).

- May demonstrate poor balance and postural stability (making activities such as biking and skating more challenging).

- May have troubles with motor imitation (making instructional demonstrations difficult to follow).

- May have a higher left-hand preference or an ambiguous hand preference (Hilton, 2011) (important to consider with sports that involve hand and foot movements such as soccer, swimming, skating, and tennis).

We know that the presence of delayed or unusual motor development might be enough to discourage parents from including their children in sports (Pan, 2008). As discussed in Chapter 1, this has implications for overall fitness for individuals with ASD across the lifespan and may compound the degree of motor impairment that adults with ASD experience. Unfortunately, there has been limited research on interventions to improve difficulties with motor-based skills for individuals with autism. Recommendations within the literature indicate that interventions should target skills that enhance the ability to participate in leisure, play, self-care, school, and social activities (Hilton, 2011). For this reason, participation in sports is the perfect context to target this skill development! Sports provide a perfect opportunity to enhance fundamental motor skills (see Chapter 4) within a functional, meaningful context. One of the great features of sport skill instruction is that new skills are taught using strategies that are ideal for children with ASD (and most other children). Skills are taught by breaking them down into smaller pieces to provide challenges at just the right level for learning without being unreasonable. These opportunities are ideal for children with ASD who have motor challenges and are aligned with what we understand about the current best therapeutic practices.

BREAKING DOWN THE MOVEMENTS: TEACHING BIT BY BIT

It is important to break down skills into smaller components for athletes with motor planning difficulties. A student with mild difficulties may only need things broken into a few chunks, while a student with greater difficulties may need a greater number of smaller skills. You may employ strategies such as:

- Demonstrating the skill.
- Providing verbal instructions on how to begin, where to move, and how to complete the movement as the student moves through the skill.
- Providing a short saying the athletes can use to talk themselves through the steps.
- Physically moving the student's hands/feet through the movement.
- Displaying a poster or visual of the sequence of steps to complete the skill.

The specific prescription of strategies that any one student will need will differ among students and are likely to change over time for any given athlete. The use of multiple tools or a "multi-sensory approach" may lend itself to engaging a range of learning styles and preferences.

4. He feels uncomfortable in groups

Many children with ASD are challenged by the social and communication skills required to successfully engage in a group. These difficulties may present in several ways:

- May have difficulty comprehending and using language appropriately.

- May have difficulty selecting and focusing on the relevant or important information (especially instructions delivered in a group).

- May have difficulty processing new or novel information.

- May become confused by group activities that are unpredictable or lack a routine.

For a start, communication and language can be challenging for children with ASD (Wetherby, 2006). Being familiar with the "Sport Talk" vocabulary to understand the instructions specific to that sport is half the battle. For a student who is not yet talking, oftentimes other communication systems including signs, gestures, and symbols might be used to help the student communicate. Does the child use a method other than verbal speech to talk? If so, it is important that you become familiar with the vocabulary of the sport so that this kind of language can be a part of your athlete's communication system. Each sport has its own vocabulary of different words and phrases that children need to become familiar with (in Part 2 we include a table of vocabulary for each sport). Some children may use symbol systems such as the Picture Exchange Communication System (Bondy and Frost, 1994). Preparing symbols that are useful in the sporting environment can help ensure that the new athlete has the necessary pictures to understand instructional language and to express him- or herself in that context.

Children with ASD can learn and thrive in groups, especially when provided the necessary supports. In Chapter 4 we'll discuss strategies for enhancing athletes' learning in group settings.

5. We tried it before and it didn't work

Sometimes you have to try something more than once. There are many reasons why sports programs may fail children with ASD. Often, there are several things that we can do to prevent problems before they occur, and to prepare yourself, the coach, and your child to be more successful in the sport. With the right supports and the right program we have observed many children with ASD succeed in sports. We share these stories with you in Part 2 and we hope that you can use them as models to try and find the right program and supports for your child to be successful in sport.

FOUR QUESTIONS TO CONSIDER WHEN CHOOSING A SPORT

Finding a sport that your child enjoys may be straightforward for some families because some kids seem to take to a sport or to many sports at a young age. For other families, the task of finding a sport that their child enjoys may be more difficult. With all children the following questions are useful to consider when contemplating which sports are suitable.

1. What does your child like to do?

Engaging your child in different activities around the house and neighbourhood at a young age will give you some indication of what your child likes to do physically. Sometimes it is apparent from your child's actions which sport he or she may like to do in the future. Does your child like to run? Some sports involve a lot of running and this may be a consideration if your child is keen or not so keen to get moving. Does your child have good balance? Trying an activity like skating or biking might be appropriate for him or her. Throw a ball down on the ground and see what a child does with it. Some will pick it up and throw it and others will begin kicking it. Others will ignore the ball completely. If this is the case, ball sports might not be for them. Also, check out all kinds of environments including the pool, the ice rink, the martial arts studio (dojang), the trail, the court, and the soccer field. You may come to realize that your child is a natural in the water or is really intrigued by the sensation of slipping and sliding on the ice. Your exploration of what your child likes to do may give an indication of what sport your child may lean toward.

2. What do your child's activity level and physical traits tell you about what he or she might like to do?

Some children with ASD have difficulty indicating what they do and do not like to do, so a bit of guesswork may be needed. We've found that understanding your child's activity level and physical traits is a useful place to start. Sometimes you can recognize your child's activity level at a young age. High-energy kids may gravitate toward sports that have the option for high intensity like swimming, skiing, and soccer. On the other hand, more laid-back kids may be better suited for swimming or martial arts.

Your child's physical traits are most often related to their parents' physical traits, so the parents' existing preferences might be indicative of your child's potential activity interests. For example, kids who are obviously going to be big or tall may have their best opportunity playing where more muscular strength is beneficial – martial arts or soccer might be a good option. Kids who are small and quick may be more suited for speed sports. Furthermore, kids who have obvious strong arms and legs may like tennis or soccer. Of course, there are often different-sized players needed for different positions for the same sport so size is not always a determining factor for choosing a sport that kids may like. Trying to see where your child might fit in is the goal of examining his or her activity level and physical traits.

3. Which activities does the family enjoy?

Almost always, parents have a sport or two that they currently enjoy or enjoyed in their youth. Sometimes an older sibling has taken to a sport that the whole family enjoys. Helping your child to get skill-specific training in family sports will increase the likelihood that you can enjoy the sport together as a family. Showing enthusiasm for a sport and having kids participate and watch their parents and siblings in preferred sports might be the path to finding a sport that your child enjoys.

TIP Plan on offering kids a wide variety of sports at a young age. Many parents only sign their kids up for the sports they enjoy and do not offer enough variety to their kids. Often, kids are not sure which sport they enjoy until they reach an older age (at least 10 years old). Of course, it is never good to over-sport kids either; by having them play too many sports in a year. Parents should realize that there is always the next year to try different activities.

4. What's available in your community?

For many families, there may be limitations to the sports programs that are available or appropriate for your child in your community. Some community recreation programs have an "Access Co-ordinator" (or similar contact person). This person's role is to let families know what types of programs and support services are available for children with special needs, and which programs might be the best fit for any individual child. Even after speaking with the Access Co-ordinator, parents may still wish to observe the program before registering their child to make sure that it is a good "fit" for his or her specific needs. Finding the right coach is often key to choosing the right program for your child. In Chapter 3 we will describe strategies that families can use to navigate their community sport options and find the right coach.

SUMMING UP

There are many reasons why it may seem daunting to enroll your child with ASD in a sports program. We realize that there are many reasons that make it challenging for families to consider participating in sports – however, as we've tried to illustrate in this chapter, many of these challenges can be addressed with careful programming and a bit of risk taking. In the chapters to come, we will introduce you to several programs that we hope will inspire you to take the risk and enroll your child in sports. We're confident that once you get rolling the payoff will be greater than the risk.

Chapter 3

WORKING WITH YOUR COACH
Parents' Corner

What you will learn in this chapter
- Ways to spot a coach that has the background and skills to support an athlete with ASD.
- A method to go about finding the right coach for your child.
- Tips on information that will be useful for your new coach to know about your child and ASD.

Parents and caregivers, this chapter is for you. The sport scene can be unfamiliar and tricky to navigate. A key connection to this scene is your athlete's coach. As a parent of a child or teen with ASD, you have had to develop lines of communication with your child's education professionals, doctors, intervention providers, etc. Now, it is important to include your athlete's coach among those involved in helping your son or daughter learn new skills.

Coaches will vary in their experience and level of comfort working with athletes with special needs. How do you know who might be the best fit for your family? There are a number of different qualities that good coaches possess that make them ideal candidates to work with athletes with ASD. We'll talk more about these qualities within this chapter. We'll also address the information that you may want to provide for your coach depending on the coach's level of experience. Likely, your coach will need some general information about ASD and, most importantly, information about how to best assist your child.

YOU KNOW YOU'VE FOUND A GREAT COACH WHEN...

There are a number of qualities that great coaches possess that make them an ideal fit for children with ASD. These include the use of a variety of teaching supports, the ability to think outside the box, use of task analysis, ongoing progress monitoring, and a passion for coaching. An open-minded coach who demonstrates some or all of these abilities is the person you need to support your child in learning a new sport. Let's discuss the qualities you're looking for in your prospective coach.

TO COACHES, PROGRAM CO-ORDINATORS, AND OTHER SPORT PROGRAM SUPPORTERS

Although this chapter is directed toward parents and caregivers, there's something here for you too. Reading this chapter will give you an understanding of the questions parents of new athletes with ASD may have when they are considering recreational programs. It may also point out the types of program supports (some that you may already have in place) that families may be looking for when seeking a suitable program for their child.

Makes use of a variety of teaching supports

What does this mean?

When we say "teaching supports" we're referring to any objects or items that the coach uses as teaching devices during lesson/practice time. Depending on your sport, this could mean a lot of different things including visual supports (e.g. photos, pictures, marker drawings), physical objects (e.g. in drills, in games), written supports (e.g. written directions, handouts for parents), etc. The use of these materials is an indicator that the coach recognizes that players may learn in different ways and that some of these strategies may help "level the playing field" (pun intended) for all new players.

Why is this important for a student with ASD?

Consider how your student learns. Does he or she learn from visual cues such as pictures or symbols? Or perhaps the student benefits from written directions to help process verbal information? Using learning supports is a clear sign that your new coach knows that in order to understand instructions, students need to see them as well as hear them. Check out Chapter 5 for more information on strategies to best support a variety of different styles of learning, particularly, visual strategies.

Thinks outside the box

What does this mean?

Here we're looking for flexibility and ingenuity when faced with coaching challenges. In these situations, does he or she demonstrate flexibility in seeking solutions? Coaches can draw on an array of verbal, visual, or physical prompts to support learning. This could be as simple as wording instructions in a different way when noticing that the student is stuck or quickly modifying an activity when learning has stalled. You might notice that these coaches are innovative with games, drills, or routines used to practice the skills repeatedly without boring or frustrating the athletes. A coach who can do this tells you that he or she has:

- *A depth of technical understanding.* The coach has a substantial level of understanding of the basic skills in this sport. This allows them to be flexible in their delivery.

- *An understanding that there is a developmental sequence to learning new physical skills.* The coach is aware that children grow and develop physically, cognitively, and emotionally at different rates and this has a significant impact on their ability to learn certain skills. An awareness of developmental differences allows coaches to modify their instruction accordingly.

- *The ability to attend to the individual student.* The coach who pays close attention to each student knows about individual differences. The coach also understands how to build upon existing knowledge in a way that meets individual needs.

Photo 3.1 Example of teaching materials

Why is this important for a student with ASD?

Each child (whether they have ASD or not) has his or her own unique path to learning new sport skills. Coaches who notice when children seem to be experiencing challenges can alter the way they explain or present a skill. These coaches demonstrate that they are paying close attention to the individual characteristics of the students. For athletes with ASD who may require creative instructional delivery to learn new skills, they need coaches who are willing to see skills or teaching practice from more than one angle, and this requires thinking outside of the box.

Engaged and monitoring progress

What does this mean?

This means that the coach is actively noting the areas where the student is making progress as well where there are challenges. This could be relayed to athletes and their families verbally or through written evaluation. Some kind of written evaluation is often incorporated within sports programs for new athletes (e.g. report cards at the end of a session). Active monitoring of student progress can lead a coach to do several things including: reevaluate strategies for teaching particular skills where challenges are occurring and alter the pace (quicker or slower) of the introduction of new skills based on student progress. Are there lots of gains in one set of skills or movements and not another? Does the focus of the lesson time need to change for this student? Can we speed up introduction of new skills in one area or perhaps there is a need to break down skills further in another area? These are all questions that should be addressed through ongoing, active monitoring of student progress.

Why is this important for a student with ASD?

This type of skill monitoring is very important for all students but especially for students with ASD who may demonstrate what are called "splinter skills." The term "splinter skills" refers to the idea that a student may show quick learning or talents in one area but challenges in another. Just like in a school setting, each type of skill or set of skills may progress at a different rate. Individualization and flexible adaptation of lesson time driven by continuous evaluation of the student's shifting needs and progress is key to learning any new sport.

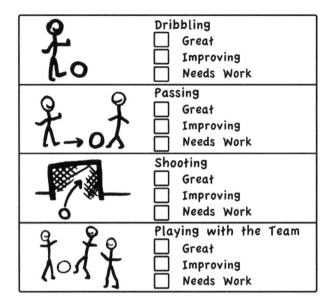

Figure 3.1 Soccer report card

Task analysis

What does this mean?

Once the coach has noticed splinter skills, how does the coach unpack the skills and activities to help the student learn? The term "task analysis" refers to the process of breaking down a skill into its smaller component parts or teachable chunks.

Great coaches engage in task analysis all of the time. In order to teach a new skill, a coach introduces smaller skills one at a time or in little chunks, whatever works best for that particular student or group of students. It can take some time for a coach to determine the degree to which each skill needs to be broken down and the appropriate pace to introduce new skills in the sequence to that particular student. Understanding this balancing act and individualizing it to each new student is what makes for a great coach.

Why is this important for a student with ASD?

Processing and sequencing a number of different verbal instructions can be difficult for some individuals with ASD. Breaking down a skill into smaller teachable chunks can be critical for learning. Once the smaller pieces are mastered, they can be pieced back together to create the larger skill. By pulling skills apart, coaches can discover which pieces have been mastered and which pieces still need some work. This process can help both student understanding and performance.

AN EXAMPLE OF TASK ANALYSIS: GETTING UP AFTER YOU FALL ON THE ICE

There are many skills that a new student needs to master when learning how to skate! One of the very first skills is learning how to get back up once you fall. This can be trickier than it seems since this seemingly simple skill involves a number of different body parts, balance, and body alignment. So you're lying on the ice, what's next? First, scoot yourself onto your hands and knees. Now, slowly use your arms and core muscles to lift your body so that you are now sitting up on your knees. Next, take one foot (right or left – what's your preference?) and step it out in front of you so that your knee makes a 90-degree angle. Once you are stable here, with your back straight and tall and head up, place your hands on your knee. Are you stable? Wait and balance. Now again, with your back straight and your head still up, push off your knee and begin to rise up to a standing position like someone is pulling you upright from a string on the top of your head. Phew, you made it! So you can see how many different body parts need to work in synchrony while aligned and balanced for a new skater to stand up. You're right, it's tough. We'll address a number of strategies to support this skill and others in Chapter 8.

Passion for the sport and passion for teaching

What does this mean?

This means that your coach has both an enthusiasm for the sport of choice and for teaching students who are new to the sport. Coaches usually have an interesting history of participation in the sport (often lifelong) and many are looking to share their love of the sport with those who are interested in learning.

Why is this important for a student with ASD?

A passion for teaching is incredibly important for new students and especially students who may take more time to master skills or who need innovative methods to learn. A passion for teaching is infectious. You can hear it in a coach's tone of voice and see it in their body language. This passion is especially important for those children who may not find sports to be the easiest thing to learn. This enthusiasm for the sport can help create a high-energy, motivating learning environment where students have fun and learn at the same time.

Enthusiasm that extends beyond the sport itself is also very important for athletes' success. When it comes to learning for children with ASD, sometimes it's necessary to take many small steps toward goals. A coach who is dedicated to celebrating each of those steps is bound to create a positive environment that helps foster the students' confidence and pride in their new skills.

OPERATION "FINDING THE COACH"

So now that you know that you're looking for this engaged, flexible, passionate, open-minded, and technically well-versed coach, it's time to take this show on the road and find this person! To do this we suggest two things: (1) speak one-on-one with the coach; and (2) observe the coach with students during lesson time.

1. Speak one-on-one with the coach

Coaches do not always speak with each family before the students arrive at their first session. As such, your coach may not understand why your family has chosen to participate in the lessons or what your expectations are for your experience. If possible, ask to speak directly with your child's coach prior to the start of the session. This will give you a chance to communicate your feelings and expectations directly without the confusion and rush that often can accompany the first day. But what should you talk about? Here are some key topics to help you as the parent or the new coach of a child with ASD, get the conversation rolling.

How do you want to participate in the sessions?

- *Parents.* Each program will have a different set of expectations in terms of family involvement or participation during class time. This will range from asking parents to sit in the stand and watch, up to taking a hands-on role in each and every lesson. What are the expectations? Do the expectations of the program and parent match?

- *Siblings.* Some programs allow or encourage the participation of siblings, even those specifically designed for children with special needs. Is this a program that families with multiple children could participate in? If not, oftentimes there are other programs for community children of varying ages and abilities running at the same time that might be a good fit. Check out these other classes if there are other children who would like to participate! This way, siblings can participate in lessons appropriate to their age and skill level at the same time. There may be options to get more than one member of a family involved, check it out!

Expectations and goals: What do you want your family to get out of the program?

There's much more than just sports skills that families can gain from participating in a sport program! Let's check these out:

- *Connections with other families.* Sports programs can be a venue to establish a new set of community connections for the participant and for their family. Some programs actively try to facilitate connections between parents during their sessions, while other programs are structured in such a way that there is time for caregivers to socialize or take a break. What are you looking for?

- *Time with your athlete.* Sports programs can also be a time for families to spend time together in a fun and engaging setting. The ability to do something together as a family may be the primary goal of participation. If so, a program that supports and encourages active in-session participation may be the best fit.

What do you hope for your child to get out of the program?

There are many different reasons for participating in sports programming, it all depends on what you're looking for! Are you hoping to expand your child's leisure and recreation options? Maybe helping your child gain social skills or friends? Or perhaps you're more interested in building a foundation of skills to participate in community sports? A combination of all of the above? All of these are great goals! The most important part is that you express your goals to your child's coach and that you find a coach who is willing to get on board with these goals. With that information in mind, your coach should be able to tailor your experience to help you work toward your chosen goals or let you know if there are other programs that might better suit your needs.

What kinds of supports could be helpful for your child?

It is often the case that athletes with ASD will require special supports to help maximize their learning during a sport lesson. It is important to let your coach know that your child may require some additional supports and provide some details about what these supports may look like for your child. Check out Chapter 5 for more information on supports for learning.

2. Observe the coach with students during lesson time

A way to get a feel for the coach's style of interaction with students is to observe a lesson or practice session. We've put together an observation "cheat sheet" with notes about what you're looking for, questions you may want to ask, and space for you to jot down what you see (see p.48).

DIFFERENT KINDS OF COACHES

Now that you know what you're looking for, let's talk about the different levels of experience and knowledge that coaches may bring to the table. In this section we'll discuss three interrelated areas that make up your coach's teaching methods and style of coaching, including (1) factors that contribute to a coach's teaching philosophy; (2) how teaching experience influences coaching practice; and (3) information parents can provide to coaches about ASD that can help coaches understand the characteristics of their new student.

1. Factors that contribute to a coach's teaching philosophy

There are a number of different ways that coaches can gain knowledge and skills that will benefit students with ASD including their personal experience with the sport itself. Every coach will have a different personal journey and a different set of reasons for why they began coaching. For example, many coaches move into the role of coach after several years (or decades) engaged in the sport as a competitive or recreational participant. This lengthy experience as a student in the sport will shape the way that that individual coaches, including the coach's personal philosophy about coaching or reasons for why the coach wants to teach. It is important to consider whether or not this particular set of ideas aligns with your family's expectations and values regarding participation in sport. A coach's philosophy can influence a number of different aspects of day-to-day interaction with students, including:

- how the coach sets goals

- expectations for student achievement and progress

- style of communication with the student, as well as the family as a whole (frequency, content)

- view of the purpose of sport.

COACH OBSERVATION CHEAT SHEET

Coach's characteristic	Indicators
Makes use of a variety of teaching supports	Uses items such as objects, toys, markers, stickers, pictures, quick sketches on an erasable white board
What you observed:	
Thinks outside the box	Flexibility – changes style and techniques based on student characteristics Ingenuity – unique teaching practices; supports the student in multiple ways (verbally, visually, physically)
What you observed:	
Engaged and monitoring progress	Ongoing communication about the child's successes and challenges Lesson content seems to change based on the student's progress and needs – new skills are introduced as previous skills are mastered, skills are revisited when necessary Written evaluation of progress at the end of a set of lessons
What you observed:	
Task analysis	Breaks down skills into small components Helps the student master the smaller components and then puts the pieces together to make the larger skill
What you observed:	
Passion for the sport and passion for teaching	High-energy, fun and positive – voice, body, expressions Enthusiasm for teaching and student learning
What you observed:	

A coach's view on sport is then combined with how coaching fits into his or her broader life. Some coaches teach part time while others make their living coaching full time. Some teach as a hobby while others teach as a career. In addition, some coaches will be interested in primarily coaching children who want to pursue elite competitive sport, while others prefer to teach recreational participants who are there to learn in order to participate in a fun activity with friends and family. This combination of the coach's past personal experience with the sport environment and the coach's future goals shape both his or her view of children's participation in sport and his or her motivation for teaching. It is important to find a coach who has a coaching philosophy that fits with the goals and expectations that you have for your family's experience.

2. How teaching experience influences coaching practice

Another important consideration is the level of experience and, perhaps more importantly, the level of comfort that the coach has in teaching athletes who have special needs. The coach's level of knowledge and comfort will shape the role that you take in supporting the coach's understanding of your child, as well as learning for students with ASD more generally.

For those coaches who are new to both coaching and working with athletes with special learning needs, the type of information and support that you provide will differ from that which you would provide to coaches with greater experience and skills. In many ways, this relationship will be similar to that of a parent's relationship with a classroom teacher. Ask yourself:

- What do I want this person to know about my child in order to help my child learn?

- What kinds of learning supports are working best for my child? (at school, home, etc.)

- What's working at home?

- What has helped my child learn in gym class or in other sports programs before now?

These questions can help you craft the information that you provide to your child's coach. Let's take a look at the kinds of information that you might provide about working with athletes with ASD for two general coach profiles: (1) the *new coach* who has just recently begun coaching; and (2) the *experienced coach* who is new to coaching athletes with special needs.

New coaches: New to the teaching scene

Although we may be hesitant to trust our children's learning to those coaches who are new on the job, there are many good things about working with coaches who are relatively new to teaching! What new coaches (regardless of chronological age!) may lack in experience they may make up for in enthusiasm and flexibility. There are many pros to working with a brand new coach! Let's explore some of these.

- *Passion and energy.* The passion that new coaches bring to teaching can be infectious and highly motivating for new students. The high affect and energy that many new coaches infuse into their lesson time can lead them to bring enthusiasm and a positive nature to their lessons. New coaches also may have big dreams for their students and for the advancement of the sport that they love. These positive tendencies can lead new coaches to think big, leading to flexible and creative delivery of their lesson content.

- *Philosophy still under construction.* For new coaches, it is frequently the case that the coach was a student not long ago (and may still be!). Unlike coaches who have been teaching for many years and may have developed a particular style of teaching and sequence to the way that they introduce the series of skills, newer coaches are still building their teaching repertoire, profile, and philosophy around coaching. As such, new coaches may be open to suggestions and strategies that they may not have encountered just yet in their coaching careers.

☀️**TIP** In many sports, new coaches have either recently completed a number of hours with or are still under the watchful eye of more seasoned mentor coaches. These coaches are those who have been teaching for a number of years and have taught a variety of levels of students. Learning about your new coach's mentor coach in terms of his or her style of teaching and other coaching qualities (see our criteria for great coaches!) may help give you a picture of your coach's experience and training.

Experienced coaches: New to coaching children with special needs

We've talked a lot about what it means to be a great coach. Remember, great coaches are flexible, adaptive, have a deep knowledge of the technical aspects of their sport, a love of teaching, and the ability to break skills down into smaller components. Since these wonderful coaches are already doing all of these things, what is most important for these coaches is learning how to identify how a child with ASD may learn differently than the athletes they often see and how they may then best support this student's learning. Experienced coaches are already making many adaptations to the basic curriculum for a range of learning styles. Now we need to help them think about how these often unconscious modifications and methods that they are already using can be tweaked to work for this particular student with ASD.

3. Information parents can provide to coaches about ASD

So what kinds of information about the ways children with ASD learn and develop could be helpful for your coach? Let's take a look at a few key points about development that could help inform a coach's teaching methods (see Table 3.1).

SUMMING UP

Your athlete's coach plays a pivotal role in his or her development and progress in the sport, as well as in the nature of the experience your family will have in sport. It is very important to find a person whom you can speak openly with and whom you feel has a coaching philosophy that meshes with your family's goals and aspirations for your experience. Remember that even the most seasoned of coaches will need your support in the role of your athlete's cheerleader and often as a valuable resource for information and strategies. Together, families and coaches can become a fantastic team for any new athlete!

Table 3.1 Learning and development in children with ASD: Things to think about

Area of information	Basic information for coaches and program staff and what this could mean in a sport environment
Core areas impacted by ASD	Understand that there are three primary areas impacted by ASD: (1) language, (2) social skills, and (3) the presence of repetitive and stereotypic behaviours (American Psychological Association, 1994). • The diagnosis of "autism" includes students with a wide range or "spectrum" of skills and abilities. Every student with ASD is different! For example, a coach may need to use different language, different affect, and different strategies with each student depending on their age, abilities, and unique challenges.
Language	Understand that students may have limited language skills both in what they can say and what they understand. • May require instructions shorter in length or more time to pick up new sport-specific vocabulary. Visual cues (e.g. photos or picture symbols) may support understanding. Students with ASD may echo or repeat what they hear. • Echoing does not necessarily equal understanding – coaches may need to check for understanding in other ways. The student may recite "scripted" lines from a book, television show, or previous conversation. • If this type of scripted language has a unique meaning for the student, families can help by communicating the meaning with the coach to help the coach understand how to best respond to these communications. The student may need extra supports to communicate. Children with ASD may also use alternative or augmentative communication (AAC) systems to communicate (e.g. picture-based systems, voice output devices). Consult the student's family for instructions on how to use communication systems that you're not familiar with. • Think about the way the sport environment is set up. Will the athlete be in the water? On the ice? Creative strategies will be needed to allow the student safe access to his or her communication system.
Social skills	Understand that group interactions might pose challenges for children with ASD and how these might be considered learning opportunities depending on the child's abilities. • Coaches can help facilitate groups that include all members. Highlighting successes, having all children demonstrate at one time or another, or help to lead activities to help provide roles for all students. • Some students might need some support to get an interaction started (cue for greetings, topic to chat about, etc.).

Repetitive behaviour	Understand that children may display repeated motor behaviours (e.g. jumping, hand movements, spinning), repeated actions with objects, or intense interests. • A coach may be able to incorporate special interests to help motivate a student. • There are a number of different reasons why a student might be repeating the same action over and over. Families can help coaches understand the purpose or "function" of the repetitive movement.
Motor planning and sequencing	Some children with ASD may have difficulty planning and sequencing movements (Baranek, 2002). • It may take a child longer to co-ordinate his or her movements and may need skills broken down into smaller components in order to do so beyond what is often necessary for a new student. • Alternatively, physical activity and movement is a strength for some students with ASD.
Supports for learning	Understand that there are a number of different strategies that can be used to support a child's learning (see Chapter 4 for some ideas around supports for learning). Program co-ordinators and families can help by introducing new volunteers to the specific strategies used in their program and the rationale for their use.
Processing of sensory information from the environment	Children with ASD tend to experience sensory information differently to many children (Baranek, 2002). They may be hypo (under) or hyper (over) sensitive to different tastes, smells, physical touch, sound, etc. • This can impact a child's behaviour if he or she is either looking to satisfy a sensory need (e.g. pressure) or find sensory information uncomfortable (e.g. lights, loud sounds, restrictive clothing).

Chapter 4

SUPPORTS AND STRATEGIES FOR LEARNING IN SPORT

What you will learn in this chapter
- General principles about how children learn to move.
- How important balance and visual skills are in learning sport-related skills.
- Ways to encourage new athletes to learn new skills.

For decades, many specialists have been studying how children learn. Our purpose in this chapter is to provide you with a few kernels of wisdom that clinicians, families, coaches, and researchers have found helpful when teaching new sport skills to all children to highlight their importance when teaching kids with ASD.

GENERAL LEARNING PRINCIPLES IN LEARNING MOTOR SKILLS

Kids have a lot to cope with when learning new activities! There are new ways to move the body that can be combined with moving objects (balls) and unusual environments (grassy fields, strange gyms, ice, or water). Through instruction, coaches, parents, and teachers can help facilitate learning in all of these environments. Good sports instruction is usually based on what we know (or intuitively understand) about the mechanical principles of movement and what we know about how we can optimize learning. Movement development parallels the development of the human nervous system and there are many factors that can influence its maturation. There are some inherited factors related to motor development (e.g. children of athletic parents are often more inclined to be athletic themselves), but in this chapter we are more concerned with the teaching strategies or the changes we can make in the environment to influence successful motor skill development.

LEARNING TO MOVE THE BODY TAKES TIME

In infancy, body movements are largely reflexive. Over time, children learn to control their bodies, especially when they are motivated to repeat pleasurable experiences or sensations. Children are more likely to develop physically when they have many opportunities to practice in a variety of environments. Through practice, muscles become stronger, more efficient, and co-ordination increases. One can observe this phenomenon in the basic movements of young children including turning over, crawling, and walking. Children start off tentatively but as their nervous systems develop, combined with repeated practice and experience, their movements become fluid and are initiated without much thought.

According to movement specialists (Lee and Schmidt, 1999), there are three stages to motor learning: (1) the cognitive phase; (2) the associative phase; and (3) the autonomous phase. We can see these stages in action when children learn new skills in sports.

1. The cognitive phase

In the cognitive stage, students are just beginning to figure out what needs to be done to achieve a desired goal (e.g. hit a ball with a racket or tap a ball with the inside part of a foot, maintain balance on a bike). Through some thinking and some trial and error, motor strategies to achieve certain goals are developed and children try them out. Effective strategies are incorporated into the child's toolbox and ineffective strategies are abandoned.

2. The associative phase

This second stage is the longest. This is where children refine their movements, becoming more efficient and effective at achieving the desired goal. It is during this stage that good coaching really pays off. Often new athletes are not aware of how to effectively make minor adjustments in body positions or in the timing of movements that are necessary for skill mastery. A perceptive coach can pinpoint these moments and give appropriate input to help the student develop this self-monitoring process and to speed up the process of improving motor skills.

3. The autonomous phase

In this final stage, children become autonomous. This means that they can automatically perform the task without having to pay much careful cognitive attention to their body movements. Trained athletes might experience this while kicking a soccer ball or swimming in the pool. It can take years of ongoing repeated practice to refine a skill to the point where the athlete has achieved this final stage of development. In most sports, athletes will cycle back through all three stages or bounce between stages as they continue to refine their performance.

FACTORS THAT INFLUENCE SKILL DEVELOPMENT

Several factors can influence the speed with which we move through these phases: stress, arousal, fatigue, and attention. While these factors are not unique to ASD, they are often affected by behaviours associated with ASD so they are important to pay attention to. Lisa Kurtz, an occupational therapist, has written extensively on this topic (Kurtz, 2007). She notes that when children are overly affected by stress and anxiety, their ability to learn new motor skills is compromised. There is an optimal arousal state for each individual. When stress is too high (often the case for many individuals with ASD), performance when learning a new motor skill is likely to be very poor. Similarly, when children are fatigued, performance is poor. Fatigue affects new athletes in many ways; they are not as aware and their visual and motor acuity is weaker. In addition, fatigue can decrease reaction time and lead to poorer execution of motor movements as well as general disorganization. Loss of attention or alertness, which is sometimes associated with low arousal (i.e. not enough stress), is similar to fatigue. A high level of attention is required in order to benefit from instructional opportunities in sports. Ensuring that you have a well-rested student who is not too stressed increases the likelihood that they will be able to attend to instructions leading to better performance when learning new motor skills.

LEARNING NEW MOTOR SKILLS

When learning a new motor skill, there are several basic principles related to movement that are common to all activities (Torbert, 2011). In this section, we're going to discuss two key principles: (1) balance and how it relates to movements in each sport; and (2) visual skill and its influence on our ability to co-ordinate our bodies with objects.

1. Balance: Start with a strong base

Being good at moving is about being able to stay in control of your body while shifting your weight to maintain your balance. This is key to agility and co-ordination during even the most basic movements, including walking. Kids who have poor co-ordination are usually struggling with some aspect of balance.

FUNDAMENTAL MOTOR SKILLS

In an effort to assist in the development of lifelong physical activity, Canadian Sport for Life (2011) has outlined fundamental movement and sport skills that new athletes should have the opportunity to learn, and preferably before adolescence. As we noted in Chapter 1, children, teens, and adults who lack these basic skills have difficulty participating in many physical activities, which can lead to decreased participation in physical activities over the lifetime.

Fundamental movement and sport skills

Travelling skills	Object control skills	Balance movements
• Boosting	*Sending*	• Balancing/centring
• Climbing	• Kicking	• Body rolling
• Cycling	• Punting	• Dodging
• Galloping	• Rolling	• Floating
• Gliding	• Striking (racket)	• Landing
• Hopping	• Throwing	• Ready position
• Jumping		(biking, soccer,
• Leaping	*Receiving*	tennis)
• Pedalling	• Catching	• Sinking/falling
• Running	• Stopping	• Spinning
• Skating	• Trapping	• Stopping
• Skipping		• Stretching/curling
• Sliding	*Travelling with*	• Swinging
• Swimming	• Dribbling (feet)	• Twisting/turning
• Swinging	• Dribbling (hands)	

Source: Used with permission from Canadian Sport for Life: Long Term Athlete Development, Resource Paper, v2, 2011.

Having a good base of support helps with balance. To do this, we typically need to do three important things. First, we keep our weight centred over our body's natural base of support. For most of us, our natural base of support is at the base of our trunk/core right around the pelvic area. Second, we can increase our base of support by widening our legs. By widening your stance, you create a larger base of support to stack the rest of your body on top of. Just like when you build a block tower, it's easier to stack on top of a wider base than a tiny and narrow one! This wider base makes for a more secure and stable tower.

Third, if we lower our centre of gravity (i.e. bend our knees) this further improves our base of support. In many sports, this position is often referred to as the "ready position" – an optimal stance to get ready to move. What is key to this notion of adding a knee bend to a stable position is the idea that *only* the knees bend and they bend forward over the top of the toes. Your balance can be lost when the alignment of your knees and toes is out.

Photo 4.1 Narrow base of support and wider base of support

💡**TIP** Some coaches develop simple key words to encourage the bent knees, wide stance, and loose arms. For example, calling this the "gorilla" is a great way to remind kids how to stand when getting ready to receive or hit a ball in many ball sports (Torbert, 2011).

In some sports, the "ready position" is great for other reasons. For example, if the joints are bent, the muscles are more engaged and the body is better able to initiate movement. With the muscles more engaged the body is also better able to exert force to swing to kick (as in soccer) or hit a ball (as in tennis).

It is important to recognize that as children grow and their body changes, they may need to learn how their new body moves in space and where their new centre of balance is located. How agile and balanced your body is changes on a day-to-day basis depending on a variety of factors (energy level, stress level, prior physical demands, nutrition, etc.). It's important that both athletes and coaches try to be aware of these fluctuations and adjust their practice accordingly to prevent injury and encourage successful practice. Across sports, coaches can help their students increase this awareness by embedding balance activities as part of warm up activities or drills.

BALANCE ACTIVITIES

Here are a couple of balance activities that could be part of a warm up routine for any activity:

- *Practice moving in slow motion.* A great game for kids, could be "Go, go, go, Stop!" Instruct the children to move slowly while the coach says "go, go, go," and freeze in position when they hear "Stop!" Challenge the children to freeze with one foot in the air or with their hands above their heads.

- *Balance on one foot.* Model balancing on the right foot and then the left foot several times. Then ask the kids to copy you. To increase the difficulty try asking the students to close their eyes and do it all again!

- *Run and come to a sudden stop.* Take turns letting the children give the instructions. They love to catch the coach who is having trouble stopping. Popular games for young children that incorporate this kind of movement include freeze tag, red light/green light, and what's the time, Mr. Wolf?

The importance of weight transfer

When we move our arms and legs we alter our body's natural base of support – this is referred to as weight transfer. For example, when we move our arms up, our centre of support shifts higher up the body. Note that the environment can alter your centre of balance as well. In the water, our centre of support is higher because our lungs make our chests more buoyant than the heavier bonier parts of our lower torso. This is why we have to almost re-learn "balance" when we get in the water.

Shifting our weight is easier to accomplish with a wider base of support. On land, this is accomplished by increasing our base of support (described above). In the water, we extend our arms in front of us, as in the front float, to stabilize our bodies and stay afloat. Mastering the nuances of weight transfer when we move our arms and legs – to kick, throw, or swing effectively – is managed over time and after lots of practice.

TIP *Understanding weight transfer.* Stand tall with your feet together on the floor and your arms at your sides. Close your eyes. Breathe and notice what you feel as you stand still. Where is your "weight"? Do you put more pressure on one foot than the other? Are you standing with all your weight on your heels or on your toes? Even standing completely still you can make slight adjustments with your body to evenly distribute your body weight forwards and backwards and left to right. The same notion applies to movements in all sports. See the "Balance and weight transfer" box on the following page for some examples.

To help children learn new movements that require a shift in their weight, it is useful to understand a little bit about the mechanics of initiating moves. It is important to remember that all movements have three phases:

- *Preparatory phase.* This is where the body gets ready for movement. This phase involves balance and stabilization of the body to prepare it to move or transfer weight.
- *Action phase.* This phase includes the movement itself.
- *Follow-through phase.* The movement is completed in this phase.

When teaching moves that require transfers of weight (e.g. kicking a ball, pedalling a bike, swinging a tennis racket) it is sometimes helpful to give the student a model or idea of what the body should look like when the move has been completed, rather than the actual move itself. What is the end goal and position of the body? For example, when learning to swing the foot to kick a ball, in the follow-through phase the kicking foot should be pointing toward the target. Similarly, in tennis, after the racket makes contact with the ball, it is extended out in the direction that the ball is intended to travel and the racket is brought across the body in a relaxed, smooth motion.

BALANCE AND WEIGHT TRANSFER

Balance and weight transfer is involved in every sport. However, it varies by sport. Let's take a few examples.

- *Biking.* Riding a bike requires that a rider carry him- or herself with the body in line from head to pelvis. Hips, knees, and ankles work together in alignment to pedal the bike. Slight weight shifting will occur as you pedal, too much will lead to tipping (see "Ready position" on p.112)!

- *Skating.* The simple act of pushing to move forward requires a shift in weight from the foot that pushes to that which you move forward on. The knee will press over the toe on the skating foot and, in order to safely move forward, the joints from the skater's neck through hips will be aligned (see "Moving forward" on p.132).

- *Martial arts.* A bow in taekwondo requires a straight body alignment from head to toe. The practitioner's weight will shift slightly forward as the body bends only at the waist to complete the action. Alignment is crucial to this skill! Only the waist bends (see "Bowing" on p.183)!

- *Tennis.* In a tennis swing a player's weight shifts from the back leg to the front leg as the arm swings the racquet through. Kind of like a soccer kick, it is very important that the joints move together to successfully direct the swing to the ball (see "The tennis swing" on p.204).

2. Visual skill

Good visual evaluation is second only to good balance when learning new sports (Torbert, 2011). We need better visual skills when we move faster or when we play with others or when we try and co-ordinate our bodies with objects. There are several visual skills that can be developed or improved during sports participation: visual focus and concentration, visual tracking (following the movement of a person or object), predicting the movement of a person or object, evaluating multiple visual stimuli, and judging speed and distance. With new players, it is important to realize that these visual skills develop slowly.

:ᗺ:**TIP** To improve visual tracking, first start with a stationary object (e.g. a soccer ball on a tee). Once co-ordination at this level has been established, you can then progress to objects that are moving slowing (e.g. in tennis, feed a tennis ball slowly to the player) or in a predetermined path (e.g. down a chute). Larger balls at slower speeds (e.g. a beach ball instead of a tennis ball) may increase beginners' success (e.g. see Photo 4.2). Progressively change the speed and patterns of the objects as the student experiences success.

Photo 4.2 Tennis racket with beach ball, and tennis ball

Here are a couple of visual evaluation activities that could be part of a warm up routine for any activity:

- *Follow the leader.* Have the participants slowly mirror or shadow a leader. The aim here is for one person or the group to follow or duplicate the movements of another.

- *Don't bump into me!* Ask the students to move around in a restricted space. Ask them to move but be careful not to bump into anyone else. Avoiding collisions and understanding body space is the goal of this game.

⚡10 TIPS WHEN ENCOURAGING ANY NEW ATHLETE

1. *Students' prior knowledge can help or hinder learning.* Make sure you consider which activities the student has engaged in before trying a new sport. This may give you a few hints on what to build on or why the student is reluctant to try something new.

2. *Focus on the preparatory and follow-through aspects of the new movements.* Sometimes setting up the movement and thinking about where the body should end up is easier to visualize than the action itself.

3. *Try to help new players understand and use the new movements through experiencing them.* Watching on the sidelines won't work. Students need to try, and try again!

4. *Show and do instead of just say!* When teaching movements, a demonstration is worth a thousand words. In addition to modelling skills, don't be afraid to help physically walk a student through a new movement as well rather than give verbal instructions. This assistance can help the athlete focus on the feeling of the sequence of movements and help him or her understand the end goal of the movements (e.g. swinging a racquet to hit a ball, or lifting the body and squeezing the arms in to jump on the ice). This type of assistance on the first try can help set the athlete on the path to developing muscle memory. Muscle memory is a type of physical learning that helps the body understand the movement.

5. *Remember that players need time to get the new "feeling" of new movements* (the kinesthetic sense) and to learn how to respond to objects of play (especially balls!). Physically trying the activity repeatedly helps to develop *muscle memory*. Give lots of opportunities for practice and repetition, this will help develop this muscle memory.

6. *Make sure you tap into what keeps them motivated.* Students' motivation determines, directs, and sustains what they do to learn.

7. *Goal-directed practice.* Practice with a goal in mind and couple this with targeted feedback to enhance the quality of student learning. Let new athletes know what they are striving toward and don't forget to let them know how close they are getting to the goal!

8. *Recognize improvement.* Even when it may seem as though it's only a small step.

9. *Keep it fun!* Don't forget that a student's development is influenced by the social, emotional, and intellectual climate of the context, so keep it fun and supportive. Create an environment the lets the students know it's ok to make mistakes and where it's ok to try again. Adults can make

mistakes too! Family members and volunteers who are new to the sport can model (when safety is not a concern) trying again after making a mistake.

10. *Self-monitoring of progress*. To become self-directed learners, new players must learn to monitor their approaches to learning. So encourage them to tell you how they're doing and give them more opportunities for practice!

SUMMING UP

Like other new athletes learning new sports, students with ASD benefit from coaches who understand the developmental aspects of learning to move. Taking the time to teach fundamental motor skills and considering the importance of balance, weight transfer, and the development visual skills is key to advancing your skills in any sport. In the next chapter, you'll read about some additional teaching tips to keep in mind when structuring sport learning activities for new athletes with ASD.

Chapter 5

LEARNING SUPPORTS FOR CHILDREN WITH ASD

What you will learn in this chapter
- Important learning supports for children with ASD.
- Environmental supports.
- One-to-one teaching supports.
- Motivational supports.

Our central message in this chapter is: *be pragmatic!* Use these suggestions as tips. From the array of strategies presented, pick and choose those that work for you, do whatever works best for your unique student! What you find "works" can change from child to child, from day to day, from sport to sport, and from skill to skill. Although we have attempted to ground these suggestions in research, there is no cookbook to teaching children with ASD. Like all other kids, students with ASD vary in their preferences, motivation, and the experiences that help them learn. We know that every child with ASD is different, and the better we are at recognizing their subtle differences, the better we are at teaching them. However, research demonstrates that there are several recommended teaching practices. This chapter will describe some of these practices to help facilitate success in the sport environment.

TEACHING AND LEARNING SUPPORTS FOR CHILDREN WITH ASD

Community coaches and other program helpers (volunteers, program administrators, etc.) may benefit from additional ideas about how to support participants with ASD in recreational settings. Students with ASD often have special learning needs that community coaches may not have experienced in their coaching careers up to this point. Through research, we know that there are some teaching strategies that have helped students with ASD learn in clinic, home, and school settings. In this section, we're going to draw upon this body of literature and discuss three types of teaching strategies: (1) environmental supports; (2) one-to-one direct instructional supports; and (3) strategies to encourage engagement and motivation.

1. ENVIRONMENTAL SUPPORTS FOR ATHLETES WITH ASD

What do you mean by environmental supports?

Environmental supports are ways that we can help provide information to students about the context in which they are learning. These supports are designed to be proactive, giving participants reminders and cues to help them understand the novel sports environment. Four broad categories of supports have been found to have a positive impact on learning for children with ASD including temporal, procedural, spatial, and assertion supports (Dalrymple, 1995). These supports are described in more detail below with general examples of how they can be applied to sporting activities.

Temporal

These are supports that help a student understand sequences of events that occur over time. Students with ASD may have difficulty transitioning between activities (Dettmer *et al.*, 2000). Visuals are effective devices to indicate the passage of time and provide warnings for when one activity will end and another will begin. Examples of temporal supports include:

- *Timers and schedules.* These help indicate the start and end of each activity. Schedules can be used to indicate the sequence of activities in a lesson or to break down steps within one activity. We'll discuss visual schedules some more later on in the chapter.

- *First, then.* Verbally and/or visually indicate the activity to be done and then the fun or preferred activity that follows (e.g. first two cartwheels then break).

- *Count downs.* Visually display how many more repetitions of the skill are required.

- *Waiting cards.* Those waiting for their turn hold a card to have a visual depiction of "waiting." This is helpful for students who have trouble managing wait time.

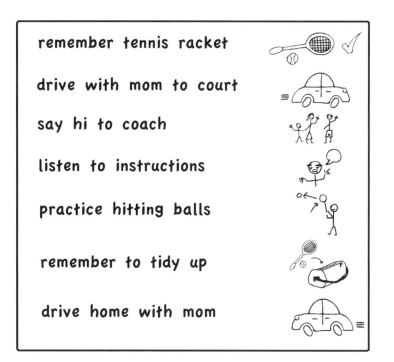

remember tennis racket

drive with mom to court

say hi to coach

listen to instructions

practice hitting balls

remember to tidy up

drive home with mom

Figure 5.1 Visual aide to prepare children for tennis

Procedural

Procedure supports depict the steps in an activity and how these steps come together to make a whole. These supports also help explain the relationship between people and objects. Let's take a look at a few kinds of procedural supports:

- *Schedules.* Visuals that depict the steps or sequence of skills that together make a more complex skill can help break down a difficult skill into smaller pieces (see Figure 5.1).

- *Rule or behaviour scripts.* Providing a visual that depicts the lesson-time rules or provides visual reminders to help cue students with tips to manage their behaviour (see Figure 5.2).

- *Name tags.* Labelling which martial arts robes belong to whom or which tennis racquet belongs to whom can help to identify equipment that belongs to a particular athlete versus equipment that might belong to the group for everyone's use.

Figure 5.2 Sit down and have a drink

Spatial

These strategies are designed to help students understand how the environment around them is organized. So what are these spatial supports, let's take a look:

- *Divide up the space.* Cues can be used to demarcate the various zones in the environment (e.g. break space, practice space, quiet space, etc.). Often, multiple groups will be practicing on the court, ice, or field at the same time. You can help mark the boundaries of your practice space by using benches, pylons, or brightly coloured ropes to create visual cues for the edge of your practice zone. Many venues have visual cues built in ready for use! The lines and circles marked on the ice, field, and court for games can be used as visually salient places to divide the space or as markers for students to line up on or gather by as a starting point for an exercise or skill.

Photo 5.1 Cones used in soccer to mark practice drill for dribbling

- *Arm's length.* For both social comfort and safety's sake, it's important that athletes are not in crashing (biking, skating), kicking (soccer, swimming, martial arts), or swinging (tennis) distance of each other! Having an appropriate amount of space between participants helps keep everyone safe from accidental knocks and bumps.

Assertion

These types of supports can aid a student in engaging in activities and social interactions including initiating engagement and keeping these activities going. Assertion supports can include:

- *Encouraging independence.* This can be done using a number of tools including individual checklists, practice schedules, or reminder cue cards that give an athlete a guide or reminder or skills to practice without having to be directed by another person (see Figure 5.3).

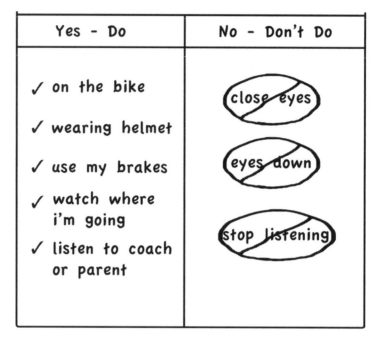

Yes - Do	No - Don't Do

Figure 5.3 Being safe on a bike

VISUAL CUES

Like many young athletes, students with ASD tend to be strong visual learners. When coaches can provide instructions in a way that athletes with ASD can both see *and* hear, communication is enhanced (Tissot and Evans, 2003). There are many different kinds of visual cues including gestures, picture drawings, photos, and physical objects. For older learners or young learners who can read, visual cues might consist of a written list of the activities rather than picture symbols.

TIP Note that the type of symbol that you use will vary from student to student depending on their learning style. It can be very informative to discuss with parents what types of visual supports have been useful for their child in the past.

Visual cues are helpful because, unlike verbal instructions that are transient (gone as quickly as they are uttered), most visual cues stick around for much longer. For students who need a bit more time to process information or who may need to refer back to the instruction, visuals can be effective supports and, ultimately, may guide their independent participation during lesson and practice time. Visuals can then be incorporated into lesson time in a number of different ways to enhance each of the four domains of support (temporal, procedural, spatial, and assertion) discussed in this chapter.

Understanding what's next

Visual supports help to let students know what will happen next. Especially in new environments, many learners benefit from understanding what will happen and what is expected of them during each individual activity and throughout the course of the session. For many students with ASD, recreational settings are unpredictable, chaotic environments where they feel uncertain about what they are supposed to do, and may be distracted by physical characteristics of the setting and/or novel items or people within the environment. The more the coach can do to make recreational settings and the expectations of activities within those settings predictable for athletes with ASD, the better.

Motivation

Visual schedules can also be a highly effective means of motivating learners to attempt less preferred activities because of an understanding that when that activity is finished, something preferred will happen next (i.e. "first we are going to do a back float, then we can go down the slide!").

Mobile schedules

Due to the nature of the sport environment, coaches may find it helpful to have both a stationary schedule (e.g. list or pictures placed in one area in the setting) and a few small visuals that they can carry with them, effectively creating a mobile visual schedule. This mobile schedule can be used to remind learners of what they need to be doing right now, and perhaps motivate them by reminding them what will happen next. Once the learner has completed the skill, the coach and learner can return to the stationary schedule to find out what activities remain in the coaching session. We include examples of visuals in this chapter and throughout Part 2.

2. ONE-TO-ONE DIRECT INSTRUCTIONAL SUPPORTS

Research demonstrates that students with ASD benefit from a variety of instructional practices. What these practices have in common is the inclusion of clear, systematic instruction. Some may think systematic instruction is limited to schooling or intervention environments, but these components are part of effective teaching in any setting including pools, martial arts studios, ice rinks, and tennis courts. Let's take a look at a few educational strategies coaches can implement during sports lessons.

Keep it short, sweet and meaningful. The language that you use when teaching is very important. This applies both to language used for initial instructions/directions and the language you use as you work on the skills with the student. Using brief and focused language increases the likelihood that your message will be understood. Ensuring that both the coach and the student are attending to the same object or activity (e.g. the tennis racquet) before delivering instruction or feedback is important too. We want the student to correctly link the language that the coach is using to the correct part of the activity (e.g. link the word "swing" to the racquet and not the ball).

-ᐴ-**TIP** When presenting instructions for children with ASD, a general rule of thumb is "the simpler, the better." Learners need to focus hard on what to do with their bodies, so coaches should keep their instructions brief and to the point!

Whenever possible, offer your student choices! These can include choices between activities, choices about what will be practiced, or even something as small as which line on the field the student wants to practice on. Incorporating choices whenever possible helps to give the student shared control, which helps him or her feel empowered to cope with the many demands that come with participating in structured sports lessons.

Carefully consider the language you use when offering choices to the student. A choice is often phrased as a question (do you want to practice kicking the ball or dribbling next?). This type of question does not include "no" as a possible answer. Before verbally offering choices or questions, be prepared to honour the student's answer including if that answer is no. Careful planning of the question so that "no" is not included in the answer list can help avoid such situations.

-ᐴ-**TIP** Remember that choices can also be offered without any language! Holding up two different pinnies (vest-like tops) on the field or two different snacks at break can also encourage a student to make a choice and participate without the demands of language.

Assisting a new athlete: Modelling the road to independence

The goal of coaching is for the student to independently engage in the activity to the best of his or her ability. Independent participation in any recreational activity opens doors for both physical activity and social interaction. It is far more difficult to engage in the sport independently if the athlete consistently needs the support of another person to successfully participate. As we discussed in Chapter 1, adolescents and adults tend

components are delivered in the same sequence each session, however, the content of each of these sections varies as the athletes progress through the program and with their individual skills.

Themes

Routines are great but we also want to try to introduce new concepts and new ideas at a rate where the children are comfortable but they also don't get bored! For example, in the adapted skating program featured in Chapter 8, each week's lesson focused on a different theme (e.g. dinosaurs, space, cartoons, holidays, etc.). The structure of each class remained the same (see Chapter 8 for session details) including a warm up, structured teaching time, a game, an obstacle course, and cool down/free time. Each of these main components of the lesson time included some aspect of the week's theme. Let's take an animal theme as an example:

- *Warm up.* Include space words in the warm up (e.g. stretch up like a giraffe).

- *Game.* For young children, games often had many physical pieces that the students had to match stuck up on the boards (in one game animal photos were dumped on the ice, and skaters were asked to match the photos to the pictures of the animals' homes, e.g. by placing a fish in the sea). This gave the students a purpose to skate back and forth between the centre of the ice and the boards.

- *Obstacle course.* These circuits included laminated pictures/symbols laid on the ice and connected by a marker-drawn path. Pictures included animal-themed movements: hop like a bunny, go slow like a turtle, go fast like a lion, waddle like a duck, etc.

Over time, as the staff began to get to know the children and their special interests, we would also try to incorporate their interests into the theme of the week (e.g. dinosaurs, numbers, space). Each week came with a new surprise theme to keep the kids interested, but included the same core sequence of activities to ensure a predictable routine.

🔅**TIP** Fun days such as dress-up days (e.g. beach day) or holiday parties can be a nice way to add in some extra highlights throughout the course of the session.

For the tough stuff: Let's work for something fun!

There will be some skills that take a little longer to master and some parts of the lesson that children like more than others. That's ok! But how do we help students plow through the parts of the program that they don't like as much? The use of a token system to encourage participation and desired behaviour can sometimes be helpful. Token systems sometimes mean earning points or earning tickets/tokens for good behaviour during lesson time, which are then exchanged for a prize or reward (Matson and Boisjoli, 2009). How much or little a student needs to do to earn a point or a token is completely up to you! This depends on the size of the reward that the student is working for and the type of task that you're asking the student to do. Let's take a look at an example:

Figure 5.4 Token system

TIP Before implementing a token system, make sure that the student's family is ok with the plan. Is there a special treat that the student can work for that he or she might receive after the session? Or maybe working for free time is motivating? Check in with the student's parents to see how you might be able to use a token system and to see what types of rewards might be of interest to your athlete.

SUMMING UP

Students with ASD benefit tremendously from direct and focused instructions, modelling of new skills, a variety of clear visual cues, and other environmental supports to help students understand both the content and structure of the lesson. Coaches should be sensitive to the characteristics of each individual child, and be sure to modify their language and their use of visual supports accordingly, keeping in mind that parents are often the best source of information for what has been most effective with their child. Most importantly, it is critical that participants with ASD (and their coaches!) have lots of fun during lessons and practice sessions! Taking time to build rapport with each learner will go a long way toward effective coaching sessions and individual skill development.

ACKNOWLEDGMENT

Stephanie and Veronica would like to acknowledge the contribution of Stephanie Jull in writing this chapter.

Chapter 6

KEEPING EVERYONE ORGANIZED AND MOTIVATED
Strategies for Encouraging Volunteer Engagement

What you will learn in this chapter
- The importance of volunteers in any sport program.
- Tips on what volunteers should know about how to support athletes with ASD.
- Suggestions on information that parents can provide to volunteers about their children.

This chapter has a little something for everyone, depending on your relationship to the athlete and the sport! As a *coach or program co-ordinator*, you'll find descriptions of the unique needs of volunteers and examples of strategies to address these needs in this chapter. You'll notice sections labelled as "coaches' corner"– these sections were designed with coaches in mind. As a *parent*, we'll provide some ideas of the types of information you could provide volunteers in order to help them best support your child during lesson time. You'll notice sections labelled as "parents' corner"– this is especially for you! As a *volunteer*, you'll find suggestions about the ways you could support an athlete with ASD, and avenues to obtain support and to share your ideas with both the coaches and the families you help support.

STRATEGIES TO KEEP VOLUNTEERS MOTIVATED AND INFORMED

Whether you're on the ice, the field, the court, the dojang, the trail, or in the pool, there needs to be a number of different helpers to support the successful participation of children with ASD. Coaches, aides, family members, experienced athletes, and volunteers are just a few of the many helpers you may encounter in a sport program. So how do we keep all these important players active in the game? It may sound odd but some of the same strategies used to support children's engagement may also help keep adult helpers on track as well. We'll discuss how to apply these strategies in this chapter, with special focus on supporting the unique needs of one particular group of helpers: *volunteers*. Let's take a look at some steps that coaches, program co-ordinators, and families can take to help keep volunteers engaged and having fun with the athletes.

SUPPORTING A KEY RESOURCE: VOLUNTEERS

Volunteers represent a special group of supporters. They are a vital resource to coaches, program co-ordinators, and families of children who participate in sport programs. Depending on the make-up of the athlete's program, a volunteer can become a specialized adult resource available to a student during lesson time. Volunteers who are paired to work one-on-one with an athlete have the potential to become the "expert" on that particular student in the context of that sport program. As such, in order to effectively support athletes' learning, volunteers need to have three types of knowledge: about ASD, about the sport of interest, and about the individual athlete they are supporting. Let's look at the information that could benefit volunteers in sport settings working with children with ASD.

1. Information about ASD: Coaches' and parents' corner

Volunteers may come to sport programs with a wide range of experience and levels of understanding of what ASD is and how it could affect a student in a recreation setting. For those volunteers that come into the program with a solid base of knowledge, fantastic! You are very lucky to have these folk engaged in the program. However, when volunteers who are eager to help support the athletes come in with little to no understanding or experience of supporting students with ASD, there are a number of areas that can be targeted to provide important basic information. As a starting point to open the conversation with the volunteer, you can introduce some of the basic concepts and unique needs of ASD that you've already relayed to the coach (see Table 3.1 in Chapter 3). More importantly, it will be necessary to help volunteers figure out how they can support these unique needs during the lesson time. Let's take a look at some basic strategies that volunteers can implement (see Table 6.1).

Table 6.1 What volunteers can do to support students with ASD

What to do	Why might this help?
Watch and notice, then respond	Research in early intervention has taught us that it is important to try to notice and respond to all of our students' attempts to communicate and socially engage (e.g. McDuffie and Yoder, 2010). These are opportunities to demonstrate that we understand that our children have something to communicate and we are listening. It also provides us with an opportunity to model new skills and shape our students' attempts. This is a concept that is important not only for language but for sport skills as well. These are our teachable moments!
Use clear and precise language	People with ASD can be very literal and concrete thinkers (Janzen, 2009). Try using clear and brief instructions. Try to stay clear of language that is difficult to interpret including sarcasm and jokes.
Watch for body language/ facial expressions	Athletes with limited language might not be able to tell you if they are tired, hungry, upset, hurt, or don't quite understand what you're asking. Keep an eye out for physical signs using the student's face and body to tell you what's up.
Be firm but kind	As with any student, it's important to set very clear boundaries about what type of behaviour is ok and what is not. Stick firmly to your expectations and boundaries but keep it positive and supportive. "First, then" statements can be a simple way to state your expectations especially for young children and early communicators. For example: "first helmet on, then bike" or "first try jump, then break."
Make sure you have the athlete's attention	Before you give an instruction or feedback, do you have the athlete's attention? This doesn't need to mean eye contact since this is often difficult for people with ASD, but is the student facing you? Is their body still or are they engaged doing something else? You'll have more success in teaching if you try to ensure that you have your student's attention before you give the next instruction. Try pausing the activity and getting face to face with the student to help grab their attention.
Give choices	Whenever possible, give your student choices. Would they like to try skill A or skill B next? Do they want to play game A or game B today? Build in options to help the student construct his or her time with you.
Get excited!	Sports are FUN! So let's have a good time! Lots of energy, smiles, and positive language can make for a good time had by all.
When questions come up, ask!	Do you have questions about a particular skill or the best way to help a student try it out? Ask the coach! This person will be your best guide.

☀️ **TIP** There are a number of well-constructed online resources that could provide the enthusiastic new volunteer with great basic information on autism. See a list of resources at the end of this chapter.

2. Information about the class: Coaches' corner

This section is designed primarily for coaches and program co-ordinators who are experts on the structure and design of the sports program of interest. However, other persons who have participated in the program who have experience supporting a child may be able to help fill volunteers in on this information as well!

As coaches, we tend to think of what our students need in order to succeed during lesson time, but how can coaches help motivate and support the volunteers and other adult helpers who are participating as well? Community members who give their time to support both the program and the participating students are key contributors. How do we keep these valuable individuals coming back to the program? Let's talk about some basic strategies that coaches and program co-ordinators can employ on a daily basis to help create clear, well-supported, and fun roles for their volunteers.

Lesson structure and routines

We know that it's important for students with ASD to understand the lesson schedule and what is coming next. This is also important for the volunteers! Make sure that volunteers understand the order of the main components of an average session as well as the volunteer's role in each of those components. This gives volunteers an idea of what they can expect and how they can be most helpful during each component. Providing this kind of basic information about the sequence and timing of the group helps volunteers do a number of things:

- Understand the pace of the session – gives volunteers a sense of how much needs to get done and the amount of time that they have to do it.

- Prepare the students for upcoming transitions.

- When working with a group of students, ensures that they split their time evenly among the athletes.

Visual schedules can be a useful way to inform both students and volunteers. Schedules can provide a quick and easy reference for volunteers to help them work independently with students. Visual cues are helpful for adults too. Check out Chapter 5 for more discussion on how to implement visual supports as well as examples.

Expectations for volunteers

Providing clear and consistent expectations for volunteers is an essential component to having effective and satisfied volunteers. Although it is often necessary to have flexible volunteers who can participate in multiple roles as needed, clear roles help define the boundaries of what volunteers are expected to do and what they do not need to do. Simple volunteer contracts can help to both establish duties and provide an ongoing resource/reference for both volunteers and program staff (see "A volunteer's contract: What could it look like?" on p.83).

When and how can they access support?

Although it would be ideal to be able to have volunteers ask questions and get the information they need whenever the moment arises, it is not always feasible to do so within the demands of the program. Providing volunteers with a venue (e.g. debriefing sessions before/after class, email, blogs) to ask non-urgent questions or discuss strategies with their peers as well as with the program co-ordinators or coaches can help foster a sense of support and community, while ensuring that volunteers' needs are met. This type of structure can also reduce the demands on the coaches and co-ordinators during sessions, allowing the focus to remain on the athletes' learning and development.

3. Information about the child: Parents' corner

The group of children and teens with diagnoses of ASD encompasses a very wide range of people with a variety of different skills and challenges. It is because each person is so different that it becomes very important that families and coaches try to provide volunteers with as much information as possible that is specific to how the supported student may learn and engage in a sports lesson (see the downloadable checklist on p.84 for some types of information to think about).

It is also very helpful when families can provide volunteers and other program staff with specific strategies that are working in other settings. These could be visual cues, verbal cues, communication symbols, routines, or rewards to name a few. For example, if families use special verbal cues (e.g. "crisscross apple sauce" to ask the child to sit down) that are working at home or at school, it's quite possible that they will work in the sports environment too! The more tools that your volunteer has to pull from, the better!

A VOLUNTEER'S CONTRACT: WHAT COULD IT LOOK LIKE?

Volunteer name: _____

Start date: _____ [insert first session here]
Role: _____ [insert identifier – group helper;
one-to-one volunteer, etc.]

Thanks for coming to volunteer with us at _____
[insert sports program here], we're really excited that you're joining us at:
_____ [insert program name]
_____ [insert program location/address]
_____ [insert program schedule – dates and times].

When you come to help out you'll be working with
_____ [insert contact person here – coach or
program co-ordinator]. If you have any questions, you can reach him/her at
_____ [insert contact information].

As a member of our program, we'd love your help with: _____
_____
_____ [list volunteer responsibilities].

Our first session will be on _____ [insert first
session here]. Please come _____ [insert number
of minutes] early so that you can get acquainted with the coach as well as
all of our awesome athletes and their families. Thanks again for giving your
time to help support our athletes, we're going to have a great time on/in the
_____ [field/court/ice/dojang/trail/pool]!

Supervisor signature: _____ Date: _____

Volunteer signature: _____ Date: _____

CHECKLIST: WHAT A VOLUNTEER NEEDS TO KNOW ABOUT MY ATHLETE

My athlete's learning and development	Check
Communication	
• My child communicates using _____ [speech/pictures/voice output device]	❏
Social skills	
• My child needs support to get involved with peers	❏
• My child might need reminders about personal space	❏
• We're working on _____ [insert social rules and skills – examples related to sports: winning/ losing; conversations; raising a hand to ask a question; listening; understanding the perspective of others]. You can help by _____ [insert strategy]	❏
Motor skills and physical development	
• My child also plays/participates in _____ [insert sports/activities]	❏
• My child has or has not done this activity before	❏
• My child excels at sports and physical activities	❏
• My child needs a bit of support to pick up new physical activities	❏
Processing sensory information	
• My child is very sensitive to _____ [insert sound, touch, smell, visual input, etc.] and it can make it hard for him or her to learn	❏
• My child needs extra _____ [insert type of input sound, touch, smell, visual, physical] to learn	❏
Way the athlete learns best	
• My child learns best when you give _____ [verbal/written/visual] instructions and directions	❏
• My child can successfully complete instructions with _____ [insert number of steps] number of steps	❏
Successful strategies	
• At home/school we're using _____ [insert strategy or support] for _____ [insert why] and it really helps!	❏
• My child really likes _____ [insert well-loved object/activity/munchie]. After he/she works hard, he/she can _____	❏

TO CURRENT AND PROSPECTIVE VOLUNTEERS

Dear volunteer, if you are currently working with or perhaps considering volunteering with an adapted sports program including children and teens with ASD, THANK YOU! Your commitment and interest in the athletes participating in these programs is invaluable.

As current volunteers may know, supporting athletes with ASD may be a different experience to working with other athletes. We would encourage you to share your enthusiasm with the families and coaches of the students that you are working with and let them know what kind of information would help you do your job. Is there a particular skill that you are unsure how to present to a student? Or, perhaps you have new creative ideas for how to present the skill? Maybe you have ideas for a new game or activity? Do you need different materials to support your student? We would encourage you to keep in communication with the athlete's coach as well as his or her family. At times, coaches, program co-ordinators, and families can get swamped and might not always be able to check in with you as much as they would like to. Your questions, comments, and suggestions are necessary and welcome, so don't hesitate to bring them up! Thank you for all of your contributions and keep it up!

SO WHERE DO WE FIND VOLUNTEERS?

Now that you know about the perks to volunteer participation and how to support your volunteers, how do you find these valuable folks? People volunteer for a number of reasons including personal connection to the sport/organization, to help those affected by a cause, and to contribute to their community (Ministry of Industry, 2009). Surveys report that over 12.5 million Canadian teens and adults (46% of the population) volunteer, with 10 percent of these folks volunteering in sports and recreation (Ministry of Industry, 2009)! Those giving their time in Canada are most frequently young adults (Ministry of Industry, 2009). All of the adapted programs featured in Part 2 of this book utilized volunteers for a variety of supports including direct one-to-one volunteer–child support during session time, group support during session time, coaching, administration, and program preparation. These volunteers came from a number of different places in the community. They were primarily university students in programs related to services for people with special needs and high school students who had a volunteer component to their school program. Other programs utilized community services such as community volunteer banks, online postings, and community sports programs/leagues related to their chosen sport (e.g. commuter biking association).

**A WORD OF CAUTION TO PROGRAMS
ENROLLING VOLUNTEERS**

In order to ensure the safety and security of children and teens in community programs, it is standard practice in many communities for organizations to require mandatory criminal and child welfare background checks from those who work or volunteer with children and teens with special needs. Your city police service or, alternatively, in rural areas, your federal police service (e.g. Royal Canadian Mounted Police, US State Department of Justice, Criminal Records Bureau in the UK) will have a procedure in place to screen volunteers for community organizations. It is sometimes necessary for the organization to set up the process with the police service rather than have volunteers seek the checks on an individual basis. Talk with your local police service to learn more about their process.

COACHES' CORNER

Keeping volunteers motivated over time

Volunteers give their time to the programs and athletes that they support, but how do we give back to them? First and foremost, creating meaningful and substantive roles for volunteers is key. Volunteering can be a rewarding and significant experience that can help individuals build skills, give back to their community, and have fun all at once! However, in order for this to happen, the volunteer must have meaningful and engaging work to partake in. Helping identify clear roles for volunteers that are appropriate to their level of commitment, expertise, and needs can help create meaningful experiences that both support the participants and help the volunteer develop his or her own skills and purpose. Let's explore some of the other ways that you can help keep volunteers coming back to get into the game!

Creating a community

Participation in sport can provide a venue for families of children with special needs to participate in their community. Adapted sports programs have the unique opportunity to help take the first step in fostering a sense of community within the program itself. As we've discussed, there are a number of different groups who may be engaged with a given sport program including the athletes, family members, volunteers, aides, coaches, program co-ordinators/assistants, etc. Creating a fun, inclusive, and engaging community can become a source of motivation, especially for the volunteers.

In the adapted skating program featured in Chapter 8, we found out (by accident I should mention) that asking volunteers to arrive at least 20 minutes prior to the start of our session helped us in creating this community feel. When our volunteers were not rushed in getting out onto the ice, field, or into the pool they had more time to socially engage with the other volunteers before the demands of the group began, and they also had more time to socially engage with the families and athletes. This little bit of extra time helped create a fun and relaxed atmosphere for all involved, which also eased the transition out onto the ice and into the group routine.

Recognizing commitment and giving back to volunteers

By definition, volunteers give their time, services, and expertise free of charge to community organizations. These individuals are crucial to the ongoing delivery of sports programs and services, especially in the case of programs for people with special needs because more adults are often needed to support the learning. As such, it is important to recognize the contribution that volunteers make to the athletes and groups that they support. Below we'll discuss three basic ways to give back to your volunteers. The more creative you can be with the ways in which you recognize your volunteers, the better! But, sometimes it's as simple as a heartfelt thank you.

1. Recognition

It is important to recognize the important gift that volunteers give to both the children and the program as a whole. Many programs include volunteer get-togethers or parties as thank you events to recognize their contributions. These social events are great ways to say a final thank you at the end of your session. Other volunteer recognition activities could involve:

- Recognition for each year of service given to the program.

- Set up a way for the participants to say thank you at the end of their session.

- Provide small treats (e.g. drinks or munchies) before or after the session.

- Incorporate the volunteers' children in the program when appropriate.

- Take the time to check in with your volunteers – ask for feedback, questions, comments.

- Recognize the outstanding work of one volunteer each month or at the end of a cycle of the program.

- Celebrate volunteer birthdays and special events.

- Have a clear procedure for volunteers to request time off.

- Give additional responsibility where appropriate.

2. Evaluation

Volunteers in the adapted skating program featured in Chapter 8, swim program in Chapter 9 and tennis program in Chapter 11 were nearly all university students in the education and health services fields. For the soccer program featured in Chapter 12, these volunteers were primarily high school students fulfilling volunteer service hours. For all of these volunteers, letters of recommendation can be very important to help them pursue their educational and career goals. Within the skating program, we instituted a formal evaluation and review process that provided written and verbal feedback at the end of each of the 10-week-long sessions. By doing this we were able to create individualized records of the volunteers' contributions. As the program co-ordinator, this was a very helpful record to provide detailed and personalized letters of recommendation for the volunteers that highlighted their unique strengths and contributions to our program.

3. Recognition by families

Some of the most meaningful "thanks" that volunteers in our adapted skating program reported receiving were personalized tokens of thanks from the athlete's families. These sometimes included small tokens such as a card or letter, but were often only short conversations expressing their appreciation for the time spent by the volunteer. Sometimes we may think lovely thoughts about those that help us but not manage to take that extra step to express these thoughts out loud to that individual. As coaches and program co-ordinators, it is important to express the value of these communications to the families in your program. Fostering an environment of ongoing communication between all of the groups engaged in the program can also help to foster a feeling of community within your group.

SUMMING UP

All in all, it's important to consider the needs of not only the students with ASD, but also the community helpers who are out there giving their all to support active participation in sport. Creating meaningful and substantive roles for volunteers within the program and making your best effort to acknowledge these valuable contributions can help make the program not just a skill-focused activity but a unique community where people get to know each other better and experience a true sense of belonging.

RESOURCES
ASD online tutorials

Autism Speaks – video glossary
   www.autismspeaks.org/what-autism/video-glossary

Educational Service Center of Central Ohio – autism internet modules
   www.autisminternetmodules.org

University of Washington – Professional Development in Autism Center
   http://depts.washington.edu/pdacent/courses/autism101.html

PART 2

SPORTS FOR NEW ATHLETES WITH ASD

Basic Skills, Strategies, and Ongoing Adapted Programs

Chapter 7

BIKE RIDING
Getting on the Road
Janine Halayko and Veronica Smith

WHAT'S GREAT ABOUT BIKING?

When I was a kid I couldn't wait to get my first two-wheeled bike – we lived in the country and it was a long way to school or to visit friends and I knew that a bike would allow me to independently explore and transport myself around my neighbourhood. My experience was perhaps a lesson in what not to do, both in terms of equipment and in teaching style. My first bike was a gleaming baby blue adult-sized monstrosity. It was so big that my dad had to lower the seat so that I could reach the pedals with my tippy toes. My older brother gave me my first brief riding lesson – he steadied the frame as I climbed on the seat, ran along with me for a few metres, let go, and I was on my own – it was exhilarating – at least for the first few moments! After a couple of spills and one really bloody knee (still have the scar to prove it!), I finally got the hang of it. A few days later I was pedalling to school and taking the scenic route home on my new wheels – as fast as I could muster, without a helmet, and with barely any supervision – it's a miracle that I made it to adulthood!

Thankfully, not all children (or parents) are so laissez faire about riding bikes these days. Parents tend to be more cautious and we generally live in more densely populated communities that require a greater concern for safety. As well, not all children are keen to hop on to two wheels – especially some children with ASD. Some children are more reluctant to take risks or need more coaching and support to master the skills needed to ride a bike. However, the many advances in bike production make it easier to learn to ride bikes today – bicycles are better built and there are so many kinds and sizes that it is possible for almost any child to learn to ride on a bike that is properly sized for their weight, height, and level of strength. Sometimes, this level of choice is overwhelming and bikes are chosen more for their availability, price, or colour than their actual fit. For some children, the fit is not essential to learning; motivation is all it takes. For others, proper fit makes all the difference in figuring out how to co-ordinate steering, pedalling, and balancing all at the same time.

The benefits of riding a bike remain the same – it is an activity most children engage in and it is also a fairly low-cost sport that the whole family can enjoy. Biking is also a great activity for children to appreciate together – quiet cul de sacs are often full of children on some form of wheels, so it is a great way to meet the neighbours and new friends. As children move into adulthood and with our greater concern for the environment, biking is also an economical and ecological form of transportation. Many cities have safe biking routes and encourage commuting by making accommodations on buses to carry bikes for longer distances (see "Resources" section at the end of the chapter for biking associations across countries).

Photo 7.1 Bicycle commuters

In this chapter, we will describe an adapted learn to bike program and provide suggestions about how to prepare your child to become a cyclist. We will describe strategies that have been successful in teaching children and teens how to bike, and alert you to some of the challenges that children with ASD might face when they are starting out on two-wheeled bicycles. We also feature a description of what learning to bike has meant to a family who has two children with ASD to illustrate the potential benefits of incorporating this sport into your family activities.

AN EXAMPLE OF AN ADAPTED LEARN TO BIKE PROGRAM: YOU CAN RIDE TWO

The "You Can Ride Two" program was started by a paediatric physiotherapist. The program has steadily evolved over time with input from experts in the cycling community (i.e. a local bikers' commuting club) as well as ideas from parents and riders who have graduated from the program. The program is run out of a city parking lot with access to a park trail system and a shallow grassy hill (we'll talk more about the ideal locations for riding in this chapter).

Who participates?

The You Can Ride Two program accepts all children who have found learning to ride a two-wheeled bicycle challenging. This means that all kinds of children have participated, including children with ASD. Participants are typically at least seven years of age at the start of the program (up to age 13), and the majority has successfully learned to ride a bike over the course of the program. For this program, children need to be able to follow a minimum of two-step directions and have some experience of pedalling and steering (e.g. on a stationary bike or scooter).

How is the program conducted?

The program is taught over six weeks, usually in the spring. Each session begins with a group "meet and greet" where activities for the session are introduced both verbally and visually. This is followed by a warm up session including stretching and/or a group game. Students are then paired with volunteers who help them practice at the child's skill level. After 30–45 minutes of practice, students take a break for snacks and drinks. The students then come back for 20 more minutes of practice and end with a closing group activity. Progressively more challenging skills are introduced each week, building on the prior week's lesson (see Table 7.1 for a description of the program).

What is taught?

Here is an example of the skills that might be introduced in a typical six-week session. (Note: children progress at their own pace but most are pedalling by Week four.)

Table 7.1 You Can Ride Two: Program description

Week	Skills taught
Week one	Basic skills on and around the bike including: • Self-safety check (how to put on helmet, ensuring shoes are tied, etc.) • Learning about the bike • Getting on/off the bike • Walking with the bike • Using the brakes • Picking the bike up from the ground • Moving while on the bike (with adult support)
Week two	Getting comfortable on the bike: • Demystifying and preventing falls • Coasting with feet off pedals • Practice braking on command • Getting into "ready position"
Week three	Balancing and pedalling: • Coasting with feet on pedals • Increasing stopping accuracy • Introduction to cornering (more steering) • Beginning pedalling
Week four	Getting comfortable with riding: • Increasing confidence with pedalling • Awareness of hand signals • Turning while pedalling
Week five	Introduction to advanced skills (if new rider is ready): • Shoulder checks • Passing others on bikes • Hills • Figure eights
Week six	Trail ride

What do the children learn?

All children registered improved in their pre-biking skills. By the end of the six-week session about 80 percent of the children could ride independently. Of the 20 percent of children who didn't reach independence, most could pedal for at least a few feet on their own but still required some level of support for starting or maintaining balance while pedalling.

How does the program help the children learn biking skills?

The You Can Ride Two program relies on careful use of individualization, clear, simple, and predictable verbal cues. Volunteers run with the new riders when they are learning to balance. The volunteers provide assistance by either catching the bike before it tips or providing physical prompts to prevent as many falls as possible. Each session builds in a predictable sequence of components which can be visually represented in a schedule including opening and closing group activities. Alongside a predictable routine, these group activities also provide an opportunity to celebrate the new bikers' many accomplishments along the way. Generous amounts of encouragement are essential to get and keep new cyclists rolling!

JOSH'S STORY

Written by Josh's father
Our oldest child, Josh, age 12, has developmental delays. In the midst of the multiple interventions and skills to be developed, learning to ride a bike had not yet been achieved and there seemed little time to pursue this formidable but important form of recreation and transportation. When Josh was growing up we lived in a busy urban area, and one of the very real practical challenges in that community was the lack of open flat surfaces upon which one could safely learn to ride a bike unrestricted by substantial traffic. When we moved to a smaller town, we heard about an innovative biking program, You Can Ride Two that offered opportunities for children and teens with disabilities to learn the skill of riding a bike. The weekly sessions, offered by dedicated and passionate volunteers, comprised many components including "runners" who accompanied the children as they rode. The runners supported the bikers in working toward the achievement of balance on the bike. No training wheels were used, just side support by the volunteer runners who brought lots of patience.

By the end of the program, Josh had almost mastered biking. With continued practice and support in our neighbourhood, Josh was able to ride without side "runner" support after about six weeks. We were all thrilled – especially Josh – that despite the substantial initial challenges with balance and the extra support needed he had learned this skill. He still has skills to learn and we continue to work on learning safety rules and responsible and defensive biking.

The You Can Ride Two program was critical to Josh's ultimate success in biking. With all the other challenges and needs that demanded our attention and time, an accessible and welcoming community-based program focused on biking strategies and support was integral to Josh's eventual development of this important skill. In looking back, this resource was incredibly helpful in overcoming the critical impasse in biking – that being the magical "moment" of finally achieving independent balance on the bike, and realizing, "Wow, this is possible!"

For Josh, learning to ride a bike has offered much: mastery, fitness, and transportation. As a family, we now bike in our local neighbourhood rather than driving, as much as weather and time permit. And for Josh, independence and skills have also been advanced. He initially took great pride in this new skill – now, he simply enjoys riding his bike like any 12-year-old!

Photo 7.2 Josh riding his bike

GETTING PREPARED TO GET ON THE BIKE FOR THE FIRST TIME

An understanding of balance and co-ordination combined with a pinch (or perhaps a dollop) of good judgment are necessary to learn to ride a bike safely. Most children are developmentally ready to engage in the physical balance and co-ordination skills involved with bike riding between the ages of five to seven, however, some children are ready a bit earlier or later than this. In this section, we review some basic information about selecting a bike, essential safety equipment, and "bike talk" that is important for the beginning biker.

STRATEGIES FOR SUCCESS WHEN EXPLORING THE GREAT OUTDOORS ON YOUR BIKE

- *Wind, rain and bugs!* There are many outdoor sensations involved with bike riding. Equipment including sunglasses, gloves, and visors (that attach to your helmet) can reduce distracting outdoor sensations.
- *So many cool things to look at!* Try a visual cue such as a bright vest on the rider or coach in front of the new biker. This may help bring attention to the road ahead and less on the passing environment.

Choosing the right bike for your rider

There are a number of different factors to consider when picking out a bike for a new rider. Bikes come in a variety of sizes with a variety of features, so there is a lot to consider. First off, don't worry about getting a fancy bike – especially bikes with suspension or multiple gears – they just add extra weight. Fancy bikes can be confusing for new riders and are not necessary to master the basic skills. But what equipment do you need for a new rider? Let's check it out.

Size

Bikes come in myriad colours, styles, and shapes but the most critical issue in finding the right bike for your new biker is the size. When your bike is the right size, balance is easier to learn. In general, children "graduate" from a tricycle to a bike with 12-inch wheels – these bikes are well sized for the average five-year-old. Consequently, for riders who are larger or older, their "first" bike may have 16-inch, 20-inch, or 24-inch wheels.

Fitting a bike

Your local bike store is a great resource for finding that perfect fit (see the "Tips on choosing the right bike for your rider" box for hints about what to look for). The fitting technique using the bike's crossbar is arguably the most popular. Using this technique, the rider should be able to straddle the horizontal bar at the top of the frame with one leg on each side and both feet flat on the ground. For beginning riders, ensure the rider's heels can touch the ground when sitting on the seat. Even when they are riding proficiently, there should still be at least two inches of clearance between the rider's groin and the top of the crossbar. For girls, whose frames may not have a horizontal bar, you will have to estimate where the bar would be to get the right size. Make sure your rider isn't sliding off the seat or tilting to one side when the pedal is pushed to its lowest point; his or her leg should still be slightly bent when the pedal is pushed all the way down.

Photo 7.3 Right fit of the bike

Other adjustments

The handlebars and seat might need some minor adjustments to make sure that your rider is comfortable. Some bikes allow for these kinds of adjustments and some don't, so check this out before you leave the store.

☀ TIPS ON CHOOSING THE RIGHT BIKE FOR YOUR RIDER

Size

Purchase a bike that fits your rider right now, rather than one that he or she will "grow into." Bikes that are too big can prove particularly difficult for children with balance or co-ordination issues.

- With the seat at its lowest setting, your rider MUST be able to put both feet flat on the ground.
- With the seat at its highest setting, your rider's toes should be the ONLY thing touching the ground.
- Your rider's knees should never hit the handlebars.

Seat

In general, the most important part of a seat is its comfort. For children who require a bit of extra help with balance, consider the following:

- Try to avoid banana seats because they are long and force riders to get on their bikes by moving their foot in front of the seat – this method can be more challenging for some children.
- Ensure you are able to firmly grasp the back of your rider's seat when he or she is sitting on it. Some styles of seats are hard to hold onto.

Brakes

Not all brakes are created equal! If your child is over the age of seven and has trouble with co-ordination, try to avoid bikes with coaster (pedal) brakes. The only time coaster brakes are helpful is when hand strength is significantly limited.

- V-brakes or disc brakes (less common on kids' bikes) are preferred.
- Cantilever brakes, often found on older bikes, are also ok but can be difficult to adjust.
- Whatever style you decide on, make sure your child's hands are big enough to reach the lever and strong enough to stop the bike.
- If at all possible, avoid long caliper brakes as they are difficult to adjust correctly.

Crossbar/tube top

This is the piece of the bike that runs from under the seat to the handlebar column. There are a number of bikes with lower or slanted tube tops. This makes it easier to get on and off the seat, particularly if riders have difficulty in getting on and off the bike.

- Lower or slanted tube tops make it easier to get on and off the seat.
- There are no advantages to having a straight crossbar. Consider other styles if your rider has balance challenges getting on and off the bike.

Handlebars

- Your rider should not have to stretch forward to reach the handlebars. Stretching forward inappropriately changes the rider's alignment and balance.
- In general, flat or low-rise handlebars are preferred because the steering instruction is more straightforward.

TIP Some bike shops have a pool of bikes that new riders can try out before you invest in one for your child. Make sure you check this out in your local community.

Protective gear

Helmet

The most important biking item that you will purchase for your rider (aside from the bike!) is a helmet. Most bike shops will help you to get the right helmet fit. The helmet should fit snugly but not feel uncomfortable. It can move a little from front to back but it should not wobble from side to side. It should rest a maximum of two finger widths above the eyebrows. The straps should form a V under your rider's ears. Make sure that you adjust the strap so that one finger fits between the strap and the chin – this way it will not be too tight. Children grow and straps loosen so periodically check your child's helmet fit and adjust as necessary. See Photo 7.4 on p.103 for the right way to position the helmet.

Padding

Knee or elbow pads and biking gloves are not necessary, but for some riders these items may help build confidence and reduce anxiety around scuffs and bruises.

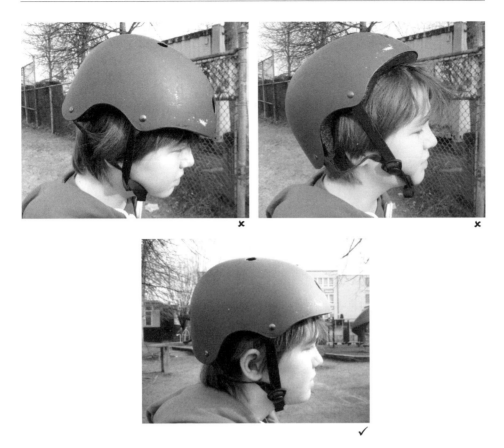

Photo 7.4 Two wrong and one right way to position the helmet

Other apparel and equipment

The right clothing

Despite the season, long sleeves and long pants are a good idea when you're starting out on the bike just in case you take a spill! When selecting shoes, it is important that your rider wears closed toes. This will prevent uncomfortable bumps on the toes or ankles if the pedals happen to get in the way.

An important extra: The bell

In many communities, a bell or horn mounted on the handlebars is mandatory. Learning to use a bell may prevent unwanted collisions by alerting pedestrians and other bikers of your approach. Most learn to bike programs devote time to teaching participants how to and when to use safety bells.

A WORD ABOUT TRAINING WHEELS

Training wheels often cause more trouble than they are worth. The term "training wheels" is a bit misleading since they do not help a new rider develop the balance required to independently ride a two-wheeled bicycle and can delay independent riding. There are pros and cons to the use of training wheels. Training wheels are good for learning to pedal and brake since they allow new riders to slowly learn these actions without the added burden of balancing the bike. But, at the same time, for this same reason they negatively impact learning to steer. This is because the balance required to steer is NOT in play when using training wheels. For many children with ASD it may be best to start riding without training wheels because otherwise, when you take them off, the balance sensation is so different that it's almost like starting all over again.

YOUR FIRST TIME ON THE BIKE

There are several things a parent can do to help get a new rider ready to bike. The following preparations are useful.

Get used to wearing the helmet

Before you get going with lessons, many children need to get used to wearing a helmet. The helmet needs to stay on for the entire lesson. It is very important to establish that the helmet must be on at all times that the child is on the bike right from the get-go. If you anticipate that the child's first lesson will be half an hour, you will need to increase his or her tolerance for wearing the helmet for this length of time.

Practice pedalling and steering

Experience on another wheeled toy before a formal lesson is a good idea. If your child already has practice pedalling on a tricycle and steering on a scooter you are well ahead of the game. Pedalling takes a certain amount of co-ordination and strength, which can be achieved on a tricycle, a plastic pedalled car, or, if your child is older, a stationary bike.

Experience steering with handlebars is also important. This can be achieved on a two-wheeled bike or scooter. There are several styles of pedal-less bikes available on the market. These are bikes with "foot rests" instead of pedals and are usually suitable for smaller children (up to the age of seven). They allow a new rider to get the feel of steering and balancing without the added complication of pedalling. For new riders who are a bit taller, consider taking the pedals off a two-wheeled bike and encouraging the rider to use his or her feet to push it along. By doing this, the rider can still get some practice steering and also get used to the motion of moving forward – or coasting – on the bike.

:☼:**TIP** How to encourage your young child to engage in continuous pedalling – for children who enjoy TV or video games, there are physical learning arcade systems designed for play and learning! These systems include a child's stationary bike that is connected to a video game. The child's actions on the bike are linked to the game and continuous pedalling is necessary to keep the game going! This is a great way for young children to practice continuous pedalling (see the "Resources" section at the end of the chapter for more information).

Familiarize the new biker with biking "language"

Preparing the new rider by introducing the language of instruction when learning to ride a bike can help to reduce the demand of learning new terms while working on the physical aspects of learning to ride. See Table 7.2 for some biking terms.

Table 7.2 Bike talk

Movements/ biking terms	Activities	Body parts	Equipment	Instructional language
On and off	Coasting	Bottom/bum	Bike	Ring your bell
Foot behind the seat	Hold the handlebars	Elbows	Bell	Stop
Look forward	Pedal!	Feet	Helmet	Turn left
Push back	Pick the bike up	Fingers and hands	Handlebars	Turn right
Push down	Ready position	Toes	Pedals	Walk your bike
Step to side	Toes under the pedals		Seat	

Familiarizing your new rider with the parts of the bike and the movements associated with biking will help reduce one of the many demands that a new rider experiences when first starting out! Use the "Bike Matching Game" to help your child learn the parts of the bike.

BIKE MATCHING GAME

Copy the images above, cut out the parts, and then let your child match and label the parts with those on the complete image of the bike.

VISUAL CUES

Some learners with ASD benefit from using visuals to support their understanding of the new "skills" they will be practicing by providing extra information regarding order of the skills and the frequency of the practice. Below is an example of an introductory lesson that includes a safety check, practice getting on and off the bike, walking the bike, and testing the brakes.

Figure 7.1 Visual support for introductory biking lesson

In a group lesson, this visual might be shared with all the participants at the start and the end of the session.

Familiarize your rider with the lesson location

If your child is challenged by new experiences, it might be a good idea to take a trip to the scheduled lesson spot to take a look around and become familiar with the location. Take a few photos and use them to discuss the upcoming lesson, this can do a lot to allay some of the anxiety associated with this new activity.

YOUR FIRST EXPERIENCE: CHECKLIST

Before you head out with your new rider to bike for the first time, check that you have everything in place to support a successful first experience!

My biking checklist

To do	Done!
Equipment check – helmet on, shoes tied, pants tucked in	☐
Bike check – tires pumped up, brakes in working order	☐
Bike talk – reviewed parts of the bike and other instructional terms	☐
Practiced steering and pedalling	☐
Practiced getting on/off my bike	☐
Took a look at the lesson site	☐
Now I am ready to start my lessons!	

Preparing your bike

Make sure your bike is in good working order before you head off to lessons. This means that the tires need to be inflated to the correct pressure level and the brakes need to be in working order. Some "learn to bike" programs will ask you to remove the pedals and lower the seat so that the riders can practice balancing and coasting on the bike at the first lesson.

Practice getting on and off the bike

It is surprising how many new riders arrive at lessons without ever having sat on the seat of their new bike! So, make sure you take the time to practice getting on and off the bike before you head off to lessons. Feeling comfortable on the seat does wonders for the anxious new rider!

BASIC BIKING SKILLS

In most cases, staying focused on practicing the skills in an incremental way will get most children riding. In this section, we review beginning and basic riding skills and discuss strategies for kids who need more support when learning to ride. Table 7.3 provides a quick reference list of the different basic skills and first steps toward building these skills.

Table 7.3 Basic biking skills at a glance

Type of movement	Basic skill	Next steps
Braking	*Handbrakes*: squeezing both brakes evenly with hand on hand help	*Handbrakes*: squeezing the brakes independently on command
	Coaster brakes: With assistance, moving the pedals backwards	*Coaster brakes*: Moving the brakes backwards on command
Ready position	While seated one foot on the pedal, one foot on the ground	While seated, use feet to get pedals adjusted, then get into "ready position"
Steering	Move the handlebars slowly in alignment with the body	Move the handlebars while looking ahead at where you're going
Gliding and coasting	While seated, push off and move forward with assistance	Push off and glide for increasingly longer times without assistance
Pedalling	From "ready position" push off from the ground, and push forward with the foot on the pedal with assistance	Same thing without assistance and keep head up to see where you're going

☀️**TIP** Some children benefit from having more than one helper, one to help physically hold the bike while the other can coach the student.

Braking

Braking should be one of the first skills taught. Before going out on any bike rides, your rider should also be able to stop consistently on command; verbal or visual cues are acceptable as long as your student is consistent. Establish the rule early so there is a much lower chance that your new biker might ride into an unsafe situation.

☀️**SAFETY TIP** Braking can be hard to learn for riders who have difficulty following verbal instructions. Even though your rider may have excellent balance, pedalling, and steering skills, the student should only be considered an independent "biker" when he or she can brake on cue.

There are two types of brakes: pedal (coaster) and handbrakes. These two types of brakes differ in important ways. Understanding the difference is crucial to bike safety. Let's explore these differences.

Pedal "coaster" brakes

Coaster brakes are slower and require less power to stop the bike than handbrakes, which make them a better fit for young children and bikers who don't quite have the necessary strength in their hands required to effectively use handbrakes. However, more co-ordination is needed for coaster brakes than for handbrakes because the braking movement (backwards) interrupts the pedalling movement (forwards). This can be tricky for new riders. Teaching the use of coaster brakes often requires some hands-on help guiding the new rider to discover what the movement feels like. This involves helping the new biker reverse the direction of pedalling and having them "push pedal back." This is easiest practiced while the child is on the bike; to physically prompt the child to stop, an adult could gently tap the bike on or above the knee, at the ankle, or on the foot.

Photo 7.5 Coaster brakes

Handbrakes

If you choose handbrakes, you will need to ensure that they are in good working order. It is also crucial to teach your student to *use both brakes at once.* Each of the handbrakes is linked to only *one* of the two tires. So, if a biker tries to use just one of the handbrakes to stop, this will only engage brakes on *one* tire, which is not only less effective for stopping but can actually throw off the rider's balance and lead to accidents. To start, new riders may need hand-over-hand guidance to depress both brakes. Remember that it's important to fade this type of assistance as the rider becomes more proficient at braking on command.

Photo 7.6 Handbrakes

A TANDEM BIKE?

Some children take a long time to reliably brake on command. For these bikers, maybe a bicycle built for two would be a good option. This way, they can enjoy getting out and about and benefit from the safe guidance of their biking partner.

Ready position

The "ready position" refers to the most efficient starting position of the pedals. The best "ready" position is when one pedal is in line with or slightly in front of the diagonal crossbar.

A child needs two main skills to master the ready position:

1. The ability to balance on the bike with only one foot on the ground.

2. The ability to move the pedals into the starting position to pedal. The way pedals are moved depends on the type of brakes on the bike.

   • *Handbrakes.* Hooking the toe under the pedal and moving the crank opposite to the direction one pedals in. Physically guiding the biker's foot to do this is helpful.

   • *Coaster brakes.* Moving the bike forward while adjusting the pedal position is necessary to get the pedals in line with the diagonal crossbar. It should be noted that adjusting the pedals is far easier on bikes without coaster brakes as the pedals can be moved in reverse!

Photo 7.7 Ready position

💡**TIP** For many new riders, getting into the ready position is made easier by doing it the same way each time. Most of us have a preferred, or dominant foot. It may be easiest *to always* start with this foot. This works really well for students who like consistency.

Steering

Steering is typically taught before pedalling as a new rider needs to be comfortable moving the handlebars to maintain an upright position. Steering the bike during a turn requires a shift in the rider's weight and lean. Gentle assistance to initiate the lean, and support during the lean, helps build the rider's confidence as he or she learns to turn properly.

DEMYSTIFYING FALLING: STEERING INTO THE DIRECTION OF THE FALL

Figuring out how to prevent a fall is a bit counterintuitive. As we move to one side, our impulse is to correct the tilt by moving the handlebars away from the pavement. This makes the problem worse. In order to correct a fall we have to learn to turn into it. To help the new rider, use a simple drill of supporting the student from behind, moving them from side to side and asking them, "Which way should you steer?" What they need to learn is that they should move the handlebars to briefly steer *into* the fall and then straight again. For example: bike leans left, flick the wheel left and then straight. Sometimes two volunteers are useful for this drill, one holding the bike and one in front of the new rider to model the correct action. This drill greatly simplifies and shortens the learning process.

Photo 7.8 Leaning into the curve

💡TIPS FOR TROUBLESHOOTING STEERING

Looking ahead while turning

Some people with ASD find it challenging to co-ordinate head and arm movements, and this can make steering around a corner challenging. If you notice a rider's bike is not leaning into the curve, it may be because the rider's head and their arms are not moving in the same direction as the turn. Often, new riders need to learn to where to look. Having a visual target about a quarter-circle ahead is helpful to get the idea of "looking into the turn."

Building up to quick turns

Turning quickly or in an "all or nothing" kind of steering where the handlebars are turned quickly or forcefully can be challenging. In this case, having larger more gradual curves for the rider to follow at first may help. Draw a large circle in chalk on the pavement that new riders can use as a guide to take these gradual curves. Once the rider gets the hang of these larger curves, you can begin to shorten the length and increase the curvature of the chalk lines to practice sharper turns.

Gliding and coasting

On the bike, kids quickly sense that if it isn't moving, it isn't stable. Moving forward while coasting or gliding will help the new rider master balance. Let's take a look at a couple of ways to do this:

Practice pushing off and coasting on the bike

This skill is best practiced on a slight down slope (less than 5 degrees) as many children don't have the power in their push off to go very fast or very far. With a long gentle slope and the help of gravity, gliding is a lot easier. Some children may need a reminder to put their feet down when the bike is leaning or slows down.

Physical assistance

This may seem a bit counterintuitive but let's say that the bike starts to lean – now what? Rather than correcting the bike back to an upright position, slow the rate at which the bike is leaning until the rider applies the proper steering input (steers into the direction of the lean), or puts their foot down. As the rider's skill develops, reduce the amount of assistance provided.

LEARNING TO BALANCE

Remember the section on balance in Chapter 4? Balance on a bike is all about keeping the wheels under the body. This is tricky because the body is higher when on a bike, so the base of support is less stable. Two-wheeled bikes are not actually stable unless they are lying on the ground! Maintaining balance while riding is the act of correcting a series of micro-falls in an attempt to retain the centre of gravity. These corrections become automatic and unconscious over time.

Photo 7.9 Coasting down a hill   *Photo 7.10 Physical assistance coasting*

Pedalling

So now that you have practiced coasting and gliding, it's time to pedal! You'll know that your new rider is ready to start pedalling when he or she: (1) can glide for about five seconds; and (2) is comfortable moving forward on the bike with the pedals on.

🔆**TIP** Have children practice putting their feet onto and off of the pedals without looking down. This is a good skill to have before they start to pedal.

To introduce pedalling, start from the ready position. This involves one pedal being higher up and slightly more forward (at around the 10 o'clock position). Pedalling requires several steps to complete, keeping in mind that all of this takes place while holding the handlebars steady and looking forward!

1. Step up to the top pedal with the preferred or "dominant" foot.

2. Push down with the foot on the pedal.

3. Push off of the ground with the other foot.

4. Place this foot on the lower pedal.

-᷍ᵜ᷍**TIP** For some riders who have difficulty knowing where their body is in space, it is easier to use their dominant foot to push off the ground simply because they are better able to master the co-ordination required to place their foot onto the pedal. Once the rider has both feet on the pedals, it is just a matter of moving forward. In the beginning stages, it is always best to have someone hold on to the back of the bike to help stabilize it, then move forward as the rider pedals. This takes patience and a lot of practice! Don't worry if your new rider takes a little while to get used to doing this independently. For many bikers, pedalling and moving forward is the last skill mastered!

Photo 7.11 Physical assistance pedalling

CHOOSING A SAFE PLACE TO PRACTICE

Most lessons take place on quiet, flat, and smooth surfaces where you can guarantee there will be no traffic (cars or other more skilled cyclists!). Parking lots, especially those beside a park or paved playgrounds, are ideally suited. If you are able to find such a spot, it is also beneficial to have access to a grassy slightly sloped hill nearby. Slight slopes are handy because some children with weak "pedal power" are not able to coast for any distance. The slope allows new riders to practice maintaining their balance while moving forward, and a grassy slope minimizes scraped knees if falls occur.

A WORD ABOUT STRENGTH AND PEDALLING

Many children have difficulty pedalling. This can occur for a couple of reasons. Sometimes it's a lack of strength and other times, the rider doesn't realize that in order to continually move the bike they have to keep moving the pedals. Some possible solutions:

- Try using "pedal cages." These are flexible metal straps that slide over the front of the foot to help hold the rider's foot in place on the pedal. They will help keep the foot on the pedal, which allows for successive rotations to build up strength and endurance.

- Need endurance to keep the pedals going? Practicing pedalling for a predetermined number of turns helps set a target to build strength in the legs – counting with the child lets him or her know that he's working toward his or her goal.

WHEN CAN WE TRY MORE ADVANCED BIKING SKILLS?

The following skills are useful to practice once the new rider has mastered the basic skills of braking, steering, and pedalling.

Figure eights

Once your rider has mastered riding and basic turns, challenge his or her balance and control of the bike by practicing riding around slalom courses or figure eights.

Hills

If you have practiced coasting down a hill, your rider should be fairly comfortable with the idea of something other than his or her legs making the bike go faster. However, it is useful to teach controlling the speed of the bike using the brakes, as well as getting off the bike on a slope (facing uphill) as chances are you will encounter these situations.

Shoulder checks

The most effective bike safety skill to teach is shoulder checking as it gives the rider the opportunity to see what is happening around him or her. Separating head movements from the rest of the body can be tricky. Practice this skill in an open area, not around parked vehicles.

Passing other bikes

Teaching the rules of the trail and proper spacing between bikes is important before you head to the trails. To be safe, riders should be taught to stay at least two bike lengths behind the person in front of them.

THE RULES OF THE ROAD

It is good to make your child aware of what to look out for in order to be safe, but teaching hand signals (i.e. to indicate turns) is not recommended until riders are very comfortable on the road. Many children, including those with ASD, are unable to properly process traffic situations when they are so focused on learning how to stay on the bike. Generally the ability to properly handle traffic situations develops somewhere between the ages of 9 and 13. So, in the early stages of learning to ride, it is best to always have supervision by an adult who watches out for safety and gradually orients the child to the rules of the road.

SUMMING UP

Biking can be an exciting new adventure for the entire family! But key to being an independent rider is not just one's physical ability to ride a bike, but also the ability to navigate the world safely on a bike. Until the new rider is comfortable with corners, tight spaces, and distractions, it is best to stick to a quiet parking lot or trail system to practice his or her new skills. Sidewalks, particularly those with sharp curbs can be dangerous and invite a higher risk of injury with a fall. The most important things to keep in mind while helping new riders practice their new skills are to: provide additional supports to avoid potential problems whenever possible; and keep it fun.

RESOURCES

Examples of learn to bike programs

Australia

Way2Go Bike Ed (southern Australia): ages 4–7
    www.dpti.sa.gov.au/Way2Go/bike_ed

Canada

Pedal Heads™ (British Columbia, Alberta, Ontario): bike camps for children aged 3–12
    www.pedalheads.ca

CAN-Bike Program (across Canada)
www.canbike.net

You Can Ride Two (Alberta)
www.youcanridetwo.ca

New Zealand

BikeNZ Learn to Ride Program: all school age children
www.bikenz.org.nz

United Kingdom

Bikeability: three levels – child to adult
www.dft.gov.uk/bikeability

United States

CycleKids (Boston, NY)
www.cyclekids.org

League of American Bicyclists
www.bikeleague.org

Lose the Training Wheels
www.losethetrainingwheels.org

Fisher Price smart cycle

Although we would prefer not to plug products, this is a pretty nifty stationary bike "toy" for young children who need practice pedalling, which links a stationary bike to a video game. Take a look at: www.fisherprice. com/fp.aspx?st=10&e=smartcycleex.

Mini glider or go glider bikes

These are bikes with "foot pegs" instead of pedals. These and other styles of balance bikes (also called run bikes and glide bikes) may be useful for new riders who need extra practice steering, gliding, and balancing. There are many brands on the market – explore them online.

ACKNOWLEDGMENT

Janine would like to acknowledge John Collier from the Edmonton Bicycle Commuters Society for his editorial assistance with this chapter.

Chapter 8

LET'S GO SKATING!
Introducing Your Skater with ASD to the Ice for the First Time

Stephanie Patterson and Vivian W. Ng

WHAT'S GREAT ABOUT SKATING?

I began skating as a preschooler. My first memory of "skating" is lying in the middle of the ice, kicking and screaming alongside my preschool buddy, who was also kicking and screaming, while our poor mothers watched on and waited for the collective meltdown to end. Fortunately, the urge to kick and scream subsided very quickly once I got the hang of standing up and not immediately falling down. I soon entered a "learn to skate" program for young kids and have been hooked ever since!

For me, the arena became a place where I learned many different social rules (e.g. winning and losing, ice etiquette, respect for older skaters, etc.). I have met a number of friends and colleagues who I am still close to even today. I also learned a great deal about my own personal attributes, both physical and mental. I gained an understanding of how my body moves in space as well as a sense of rhythm and movement that have both lent themselves to participation in other sports as well as recreation activities. More importantly, I learned about some of my own strengths and challenges in managing my own mind, as skating (like many sports) is often more of a mind game than a physical one.

Over time, skating became a much-needed activity where I could experience release and relaxation from the demands of life that came along through the teen years and onward. The ice became a safe place where my mind and body could be freed for 60 minutes or so at a time. Relaxing through physical exertion may seem odd. There is a certain freedom that comes along with movement that feels natural and purposeful as the wind whisks by your face on a clean sheet of ice. This is the kind of journey that sport can inspire. We hope to help spark a love for sport and the start of many new individual journeys in this chapter.

SO WHY SKATING?

In North America, skating is a popular community pastime for many children and families. In Canada, skating is often included as part of physical education in schools. Learn to skate programs that teach basic introductory skating skills for people of all ages exist in many countries. In Canada, over 125,000 young skaters have been enrolled in the nation's learn to skate program "CanSkate"™ offered through Skate Canada figure skating clubs across the country (see "Resources" section at the end of the chapter for a variety of programs across the world).

In the United States, over 100,000 skaters are enrolled in over 900 clubs offering the United States Figure Skating Association's "Basic Skills" program. It's not only through learn to skate programs that people worldwide are participating in sports on skates, however. The International Ice Hockey Federation reported in a survey from 2009 that just under 500,000 Canadians were registered players. In addition, there are over 465,000 registered ice hockey players in the United States and many players are registered throughout Europe, Asia, and Africa. Hockey and figure skating are just two examples of the many different avenues in both individual and group sports that one can follow once basic skating skills have been mastered. Other options include speed skating and synchronized skating. There are many sport and recreation options for a child who can skate!

BENEFITS OF SKATING

One of the great things about learn to skate programs is that children are able to move through these programs at their own pace. This helps to accommodate a range of different rates of skill development and learning. Although challenging, a great perk to skating is learning to understand where each component of one's body is in space. Children with ASD often experience difficulties with motor co-ordination (Baranek, 2002; see Chapter 4 for more discussion of motor planning and strategies for success). However, skating can prove to be a venue through which children can also learn to: (1) monitor their body parts: (2) monitor their movement; and (3) sequence different movements.

In this chapter we'll explore the potential benefit of the skating environment and how best to support children on the autism spectrum on the ice. We'll also help you prepare your new skater for your first on-ice adventure by walking you through fundamental basic skating skills and providing preparatory plans as well as on-ice strategies to help you engage in a smooth, exciting, and successful first introduction to skating!

STRATEGIES FOR SUCCESS IN THE ARENA

- *A little too attracted to the ice and snow?* Try freezies or popsicles on the ice to provide "cool" oral sensations while upright!
- *Are the sounds of blades and voices echoing a bit much?* Try some noise buster headphones for a quiet experience.
- *Eeek, this is too tight!* Is the equipment rubbing or squeezing your student in a funny way? Try putting a barrier between the skater and the equipment (e.g. toque or knit hat under the helmet, thicker socks in the skates). Also, remember that many figure skates can be "punched out" to allow more room in certain areas of the skate that may rub or feel too tight on your foot.
- *Yikes, it's bright in here!* Grab a pair of shades or tinted glasses before you step out onto the ice.

AN EXAMPLE OF AN ADAPTED LEARN TO SKATE PROGRAM FOR CHILDREN AND TEENS WITH ASD

For four years, the authors of this chapter have run a learn to skate program serving families of children and teens with ASD in Alberta, Canada. We provide a description of the structure of this program to help coaches and families generate ideas and methods that may work in their communities.

Who participates?

Sixty families with children of all ages (3–15 years) and levels of ability have participated in this program over the course of several years. The group typically includes 6–10 children diagnosed with ASD and two or three typically developing community children. Parents, aides, and volunteers provide individual support for children while they are on the ice.

Where and when do they skate?

Participants skate once a week for 8–12 weeks per session. A local community figure skating club has included the program in their schedule so our group runs on the same ice surface alongside four or five other community groups.

What do the skaters learn?

Children have learned at different rates and mastered different skills including the basic skills described in this book as well as much more! As we are in Canada, the skaters learned the same skills delivered in Skate Canada's national program CanSkate™. On average, over the course of an 8–12-week session, children mastered the basic skills that we describe in this chapter (see "Basic skating skills" section). Children who enrolled in more than one session were exposed to more advanced skills, with skaters learning basic hockey or figure skating skills.

In order to encourage independent skating skills, no physical props were permitted on the ice to help the children stand (e.g. chairs, metal bars, sleds). We recommend that these props be used with extreme caution because they can cause injury if children fall onto them or crash into other skaters or objects (e.g. the boards).

How does the program help the students learn skating skills?

Each lesson is 45 minutes long and includes the same six components each week, however, depending on the age and ability of the children, the amount of time spent on each component and the skills taught differs. Take a peek at Table 8.1 to see how we put our sessions together.

Why do we need alternative delivery methods such as this one?

Community learn to skate programs often involve some of the same structure including a group warm up, structured teaching time, and game time. However, in our program we use many of the supports mentioned in Chapter 5 including a variety of visual supports and creative methods to incorporate greater repetition (e.g. extra review/individual practice time, skill circuits with picture symbols, etc.) than are usually provided in community programming. Visual supports are infused throughout the sessions including: (1) a visual schedule of the session (group and individuals' schedules); (2) visual (picture and symbol) instructions for games; and (3) a skill circuit using picture symbols placed on the ice. Overall, an adapted learn to skate program can provide a safe and fun environment for new skaters to develop a solid foundation of skating skills to help propel them into recreational skating, figure skating, or hockey.

Table 8.1 Session breakdown and description

Program components	Description
Group warm up (5–7 minutes)	This includes stroking around the arena, a bit of social time with peers as well as group stretching.
Review (5 minutes)	Review the skills that the skaters have learned thus far (e.g. marching, hop, backward stepping) either via a game, activity, or structured teaching depending on age and ability of participants.
Structured teaching (10–15 minutes)	In a circle or on a line, the children are introduced to new skills or return to skills that have yet to be mastered (e.g. stop, push, jump). Adults support the children one on one, helping them attend to the instructor and attempt the skills.
Game (5–10 minutes)	A simple game using one or more of the skills they were just introduced to – the game varies depending on the age of the participants (e.g. red light, green light, what's the time, Mr. Wolf? for groups of younger children; more practice in pairs and small groups for older skaters).
Symbol/ picture circuit (10 minutes)	A trail of marker dots on the ice leading to different themed symbols or pictures (e.g. transportation theme: stop sign for stop, yield for glide, bumps for jump, etc.). A poster-sized legend of what each symbol means is placed on the boards. Skaters review the meaning of the symbols as a group and then disperse to try out the circuit.
Free time and cool down (5 minutes)	Participants have time to play around, practice and do what they like on the ice, ending the session on a positive note.

GETTING PREPARED TO GET OUT ON THE ICE FOR THE FIRST TIME

Your first experience on the ice as a new skater (or the parent of a new skater!) can feel a bit overwhelming. Trying to sort out the new equipment, the new environment, and the new demands on your body can be a lot to handle! Let's take a moment to explore this new experience and consider how one might support a new skater with ASD before arriving at the arena.

Equipment

There are four different key types of equipment that a skater needs in order to be comfortable and safe on the ice.

Photo 8.1 Visual supports used on the ice

Skates

Although renting skates can be a great way to first try out skating, rental skates are often of poor quality and ill-fitting which can make skating much more difficult and uncomfortable than it should be! If possible, obtaining good-quality single-blade starter hockey or figure skates (ranging from C$50–100 for a child under the age of six) is a worthy investment. Quality second-hand skates can often also be purchased through skate-specific retailers, many of whom provide a consignment process in order for families to sell skates that children have grown out of or no longer use. Quality retailers can help you determine your skate size. Note that your shoe size isn't the same as your skate size.

⌖TIP Does your skater have sensitive feet? Quality figure skates are often made of materials that are designed to be heated and then moulded to the foot of the skater. This creates a fit that adjusts somewhat to the unique ridges of a skater's foot. This is a good option for those skaters who have very sensitive feet! But, also keep in mind that this can make second-hand quality skates a bit of an awkward fit at times so you may have to try on several second-hand pairs before you find the right ones for you.

DAVID'S STORY: THE ROAD TO THE NHL IS ICY, BETTER LEARN TO SKATE

Don Kwas

David, my 13-year-old son with autism had been on skates a couple of times during family outings and physical education classes at school with mixed success. However, we knew from some of his other activities that he had good balance, an important part of successful skating. When we heard of a skating program for kids with autism, we figured we'd give skating another try. As kids, I'd played hockey and my wife figure skated, like most other kids growing up on the Canadian Prairies. We wanted our sons to enjoy skating as much as we did and thought it might provide some foundational skills for hockey.

This time around, we used several strategies to help David succeed on the ice. For example, we were able to use the time driving to the arena to prepare David for each lesson. We talked about who we would see, what we might do, and where we would go for a snack afterwards if he did a great job and tried his best!

David really enjoyed being in the cold air in the arena and loved picking up the snow in his hands. Of course, our biggest ongoing challenge was to keep him from putting it in his mouth! At first, we had to be really attentive to verbally prompt him to keep the snow from his mouth. Over time, he became much better at self-managing this behaviour. The group was fun and included a number of games that the kids could play to help them practice their skating skills. David had a great time at the lessons and learned a number of skills including skating backwards, stopping (before crashing into the boards!), turning and jumping in both directions, and crossovers to gain speed. Not only did he get to work on his own skills, but he got to participate with other kids of varying skill levels in all sorts of group activities, often becoming a model for the younger, less experienced skaters.

Skating turned out not only to be fun and beneficial for David, but for our family as a whole. I accompanied David out on the ice as his aide, so I got to work on improving my skating, too. We also had fun as a family including David's older sister, Brittany, and younger brother, Eric, in the lessons. At the lesson we met up with other families who David knew from other group activities, so it turned out to be a bit of a support group. All of these factors led us to continue to participate in skating lessons for three years. Today, David still skates in school with his peers and in the community with his family.

Photo 8.2 David

Helmet

A helmet (hockey or snowboarding are most appropriate) can also be purchased from sporting goods retailers. It's important to note that helmets come in different sizes and, again, your skater's head should be measured before purchasing a helmet.

:🔆:**TIP** If your child is particularly sensitive to garments touching his or her skin, sometimes the use of a barrier such a toque/knit cap under the helmet or thicker socks in the skates can help to reduce feelings of irritation on the skin. This is because there is less movement between the child's head/feet and the helmet/skates.

Mittens/gloves

Protection from the cold and from other skate blades is a must for little hands! The most important feature of a mitten is that it be waterproof. For new skaters who will likely start by spending more time sitting than standing on the ice, keeping the hands safe, dry, and warm is key! Lightweight waterproof mitts are your best bet.

Lightweight waterproof clothing

Light layers that allow the skater to move and bend are best. Skaters quickly create heat once they begin to move so snowsuits are often too hot and bulky. Fleece tops and pants underneath nylon jackets and pants are great for beginners.

:🔆:**TIP** Now that we have identified the main pieces of equipment that you will need on the ice (skates, helmet, mittens/gloves, and light waterproof clothing), how might you introduce this new apparel to your skater? Many children with ASD have sensitivities to touch and pressure (Jasmin *et al.*, 2009) that might make skating equipment less comfortable for them. Trying on your skates (with skate guards on!) and helmet while the child is comfortable and relaxed at home can act as a test run and help your child to feel comfortable in the new apparel. This test run also helps new skaters adjust their balance and become comfortable supporting their feet on the skate blade.

ON-ICE ETIQUETTE

Are you or another family member, aide, or teacher planning to head out onto the ice to help support your new skater? This is a great idea! But, don't forget: proper skating equipment is a must, not only for the athlete, but for the *adults* who accompany him or her out onto the ice. If you will be on the ice, you *must* be on skates for the safety of all who are on the ice. Helpers will not be allowed onto the ice surface without skates. Gloves and waterproof pants are also a good idea so that you will be comfortable sitting down on the ice with your new skater to support first attempts to get up and down from the ice surface. Check with your coach regarding registration and safety requirements for adult helpers who plan to come out onto the ice.

Practice basic skills

One of the most basic but most important skills and concepts that new skaters will be introduced to during a skating lesson is the process of falling down and then getting back up. Many young children benefit from practicing this off the ice first. By doing this, the child can get used to both the sequence of motor movements required to get up as well as the language used. It might be helpful to identify and label important body parts (e.g. knees, feet, legs, hands) with words and/or pictures.

(a)   *(b)*   *(c)*

Photo 8.3 Get up

> 💡**TIP** Let's practice! Start standing up, then crumple your body to the ground till you are sitting. To stand up, start by sitting up on your knees (kneeling). Then lift up one leg so your foot is planted on the floor and your knee is at a 90-degree angle. Now use your hands to push off the floor or your knee to stand up.

Familiarize yourself with "skating talk"

The movements and skills associated with skating have a number of different labels that are probably novel to any new skater! Table 8.2 provides some examples of skating vocabulary. Let's check it out.

Table 8.2 Skate talk

Movements	Body parts	Equipment	Other terms
Skate/push	Feet	Skates	Boards
Backwards	Knees	Helmet	Break
March	Legs	Mittens	Dressing room
Hop/jump	Hands	Jacket	Fall down/get up
Spin	Tummy	Pants	Erase (for stopping)
Stop		Socks	Help
Stroking			Ice
Turn			Warm up

VENTURING OUT ONTO THE ICE FOR THE FIRST TIME

Give yourself a bit of extra time at the arena before your first scheduled session. Often parents will need to fill out a bit of paperwork before the new skater can get out on the ice. Extra time will also provide an opportunity for the child to explore the arena, meet their coach, and get their gear on.

Are you ready to get on the ice now? Let's take a look at the ways in which you can support a new skater in these important first moments of his or her journey on the ice.

Support first steps

Imagine, after having mastered walking around the house wearing skates, you step on to the ice for the first time and then you feel your feet slide out from under you. What just happened? That was scary!

The first steps onto the ice can be a scary experience for many new skaters, young and old alike! Having a capable skater stand in front of the new skater and hold his or her hands as the first steps onto the ice are taken can help in a couple of ways: (1) by providing a sense of safety and encouragement; and (2) by providing some physical support if needed. Although learning to fall and get back up is an essential basic skill, preventing a negative association between the first experience on the ice and falling, will help to decrease feelings of apprehension and anxiety and create a positive first moment.

Initial physical support can help get the new skater started but of course you can't hold the skater up forever! Try supporting your child by the hands or from behind (holding him or her under the armpits) for his or her first 10 steps then gently help the child sit on the ice. I hope you brought warm pants because this is a great time to sit down with your child! Your child may want some time to visually explore the ice or touch the ice surface. When you're both ready, try introducing the action of standing up using the same steps you already tried at home. You can help your child by providing physical supports (holding hands). Once your child is experiencing some success, immediately start to fade the amount of physical help you provide.

(a)   (b)

Photo 8.4 Physical assistance

CAUTION

Physically supporting a new skater on the ice *can be very physically taxing for the helper.* It is very important that helpers feel secure and confident in their own skating abilities before physically helping a beginner. If you are unsure of your balance or skill level, it is worth trying out a couple of free public skating times by yourself before trying to assist a new skater. If in doubt, be conservative and consider seeking help from a more seasoned skater.

TIP A gentle next step in fading your physical assistance can be the use of your pointer finger rather than your hand to assist the child in standing. You're right if you're thinking "that doesn't sound like it would help." You can't provide a lot of lifting support just with your finger, it's used more as a confidence booster for children who are nearly standing independently but don't feel comfortable completing the action all by themselves just yet.

Standing on the ice can be really tough for many young skaters! Some children are able to progress quickly from needing support to stand on the ice to moving around the ice independently, while others are more anxious about losing the sense of safety that comes with holding onto another person. Here's an example of a child who was participating in the authors' group learn to skate program.

MARK'S STORY: GAINING CONFIDENCE

Mark was a child who possessed the ability to skate on his own but lacked the confidence to attempt this on his own. If given the choice, he would grip onto the adult with both hands and not let go. What we did was distance the adult from Mark so that he had access to holding onto both of her hands but not the rest of her body. This assistance was then faded to providing access to only one hand. At this point, Mark was still using both of his hands to hold onto the adult's single hand. In order to progress toward skating independently, Mark needed to become comfortable with skating while having both hands free. Mark's parents brought a familiar stuffed toy to the rink to help comfort their son. We used the toy to help create distance between Mark and the adult. To do this, Mark held one side of the toy and the adult held the other. This allowed Mark to still feel a sense of connection with the adult while eliminating the physical connection between them. This process took time but soon enough Mark was able to take his first few strides on the ice without seeking any support from any adults or other physical object.

YOUR FIRST EXPERIENCE: CHECKLIST

Do you have everything you need for your first day on the ice? Look through the checklist below: is there anything you're missing?

My skating checklist

To do	Done!
Equipment check – skates, helmet, mittens and light waterproof clothing	❏
Adult helpers – equipment – skates, mittens, waterproof clothing (helmet if required)	❏
Try out equipment at home	❏
Visuals and symbols for skating	❏
Sensory items for on the ice (e.g. chewy tube or freezies; glasses)	❏
Explore the rink	❏
Meet the coach	❏
Warm up – practice off the ice	❏

Now I'm ready to go skating! Remember to take off your skate guards before stepping on the ice!

BASIC SKATING SKILLS

Learn to skate programs are typically overseen by a country's national skating organization (see "Resources" section for a list of countries and their associated sporting bodies). Although each program has its own structure and terminology, there are several basic skills that every young skater will be introduced to. For children who have no prior skating experience and are around the age of six, they would typically be placed in an introductory program designed to help children learn basic skills through games and fun activities. There are several different forms of movement, each with its own basic skills (see Table 8.3 for a quick reference list). Types of movement can include stepping/pushing both forward and backward, gliding, twisting, and stopping motions.

Moving forward

Let's talk a little bit more about each of these basic skating skills, starting with the *stepping/pushing forward movement.* Stepping or marching is the first step to movement on the ice. It is typically easier for new skaters to find their balance while moving with small steps first. Once a child has mastered moving forward using a stepping action (10 steps without falling), you can begin to introduce a pushing action where the skater alternates pushing slightly to the side and back with one foot then the other. It is often more difficult to maintain one's balance while pushing vs. stepping, however, pushing allows for more speed and fluid movement.

Table 8.3 Basic skating skills at a glance

Type of movement	Basic skill	Next steps
Stepping/pushing forward	Stepping/walking forward Marching	Push and glide forward
Stepping/pushing backward (bwd)	Stepping/walking backward	Push and glide backward
Gliding	Gliding forward on two feet	Gliding forward on two feet then one foot
	Gliding backward on two feet	Gliding backward on two feet then one foot
Stopping	Push foot back and forth to make a snow pile	Push foot out to side while moving to stop (snow plow stop)
Twisting and turning	Twisting on the spot	Turn forward to backward on the spot
Hopping	Hop on two feet on the spot	Hop on two feet going forward
Spinning	Walk/march in a circle	Bend the knees over the toes and wind arms counterclockwise to start spin action

Back it up!

Similarly, stepping/pushing can be used for *backward movement*. Again, stepping while moving slowly backward is a basic skating skill.

💡**TIP** standing face to face or side by side and holding the child's hands can help to provide the child with extra stability, and help encourage an initial sense and understanding of the difference between forward and backward movement. See p.130 for a description and photos depicting methods to physically assist a new skater.

(a)   (b)

Photo 8.5 Pushing action

Gliding

The act of gliding on the ice refers to a motion where the body is still but travelling across the ice. Gliding is first done on two feet and can be useful for pausing, resting, or regaining balance. Gliding can provide an opportunity to introduce body parts and help a child understand how the components of their body line up before the tricky moves are involved! Visuals and peer models can be used to help show a child both how to stand and help point out important body parts (see Chapter 5 for more strategies for learning).

TIP When you are new to the ice, it is easy for one's body parts to get out of synch! When this happens, falling is much more likely. New skaters may need reminders to "stop" their body and glide in order to regain their balance to keep from falling. The "quieter" a young skater can make his or her body, the more successful he or she will be with balance.

Once you have mastered gliding on two feet, you can try this out on one foot! Begin by gliding forward with some momentum on two feet, once you feel balanced and steady, try gently lifting one foot up off the ice and slightly behind you by bending this leg at the knee (*technical terms:* we call the leg that is in the air your "free leg" and the one that is on the ice your "skating leg").

Photo 8.6 Gliding

Photo 8.7 David gliding on one foot

Stopping

Now that the skater is able to move forward, for the skater's safety, it's equally important to learn how to *stop* this motion. Stopping can be tricky because it requires a fair bit of balance. "Erasing" characters that are drawn on the ice with markers can act as an introduction to stopping. Standing on the spot with a slight bend in the knees, press one foot outward (to the side) over the drawing and then pull the foot back toward the body to "erase" the mark on the ice.

TIP Make use of the skater's new gliding skills to steady the body and start to slow the speed of the motion before pressing the foot out to stop.

Twisting and turning

These types of skills can involve moving portions of the body (e.g. twisting at the waist) or turning the entire body (e.g. turning from forward to backward).

Photo 8.8 Turn

Turning one's body to face another direction can be one of the more challenging skills a new skater will learn because it can be difficult to maintain balance while turning. Twisting on the spot (like the dance!) is a great way to start. When introducing twisting, emphasis on a slight bend (30 degrees) in the knees and standing up tall is important. Once the skater becomes comfortable twisting on two feet on the spot, moving forward can be introduced. Teaching turning while moving forward or backward involves the use of two of the other skills that have already been introduced: (1) stepping/pushing forward; and (2) gliding. Now you can add turning! Start off slowly to help the new skater keep control of his or her body. Try taking two or three steps forward followed by a two- to three-second glide, ending with a turn to backward.

─────────────────────────────

☆ **TIP** Knee bending is particularly important for twisting and turning. Introducing a child to the meaning of "bending your knees" (i.e. how much, how the rest of the body should be aligned) will make the introduction of turning flow more smoothly.

─────────────────────────────

Hopping

Hopping or jumping involves lifting the body off the ice. Again, the simplest way to begin is to start standing still on the spot and work on moving the body parts in order. Start big with your feet hip-distance apart and your arms out to the side or making a reverse "L" shape (see Photo 8.9a).

Next, bend the knees over the toes while keeping the arms out and standing tall and straight. Then we're going to pull all these body parts together. As you slowly pull up in the knees, squeeze the arms into the chest and push off the ice gently with your feet (see Photo 8.9b). Last, attempt to land the hop with a slight knee bend, bringing arms out to the side to steady your balance (see Photo 8.9c).

Once a new skater has mastered his or her balance while hopping on the spot, you can introduce hopping while moving forward. This is simplest if you start slowly with two or three steps or pushes, then a short glide, then the hop.

─────────────────────────────

☆ **TIP** Particularly important for hopping, is the co-ordination of bringing the arms into the chest and jumping upward. Begin with arms out and knees bent. When the skater's body is still and steady, pull up in the knees and bring the arms in to jump.

─────────────────────────────

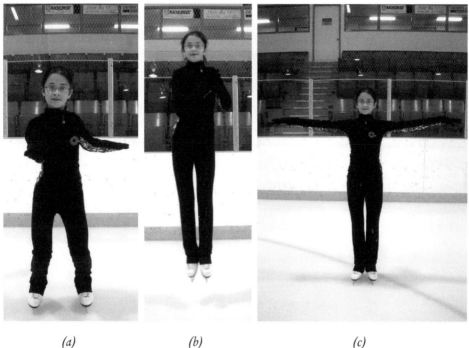

(a)   (b)   (c)

Photo 8.9 Jump – 1, 2, 3

Spinning

This skill involves some of the same motions that you have learned as part of both twisting and turning, as well hopping.

🔆 **TIP** Spinning can be slow to start and that's ok! It's tough to synchronize all the different pieces of the body to create the spinning motion. The important thing here is to *slow* things down and make sure that all the body parts are moving at the *same* time to initiate the spin. Over time, the skater will be able to put more physical force behind the initiation of this action and to really spin well, a skater will eventually move into a spin position with momentum rather than standing still on the spot… We'll share a secret, it's *way* easier to spin once you are initiating a spin from another movement, this will come a bit later on so be patient when it comes to spinning.

Just like in hopping, start big with your feet spread hip-distance apart and your arms out to the side (see Photo 8.10a). Then, we're going to bend the knees over the toes and wind the arms in the opposite direction of your spin rotation (note: most people rotate counterclockwise so your arms would be placed in a clockwise direction around the body; see Photo 8.10b).

Last, it's time to pull all these body parts together to create the spin motion. Altogether now, squeeze the feet together as you gently pull up in the knees and squeeze the arms into the chest (see Photo 8.10c). You're spinning!

(a)   (b)   (c)

Photo 8.10 Spin – 1, 2, 3

WHEN CAN WE TRY MORE ADVANCED SKATING SKILLS?

This question is best answered by a certified skating coach. Once the new skater has mastered the basic skills presented in this chapter, he or she should be able to: independently step/skate forward 10–20 consecutive steps without falling, step or wiggle backward, walk in a circle, hop on the spot, twist and turn on the spot, and make a stopping action. For those who may be apprehensive about trying skating, this set of skills would be a very solid base from which a child could enter community-based lessons. Perhaps your skater is already participating in a skating program for athletes with special needs. Is there a point when your skater could be ready to move into the regular community programs? Yes of course! But this transition can be a bit tricky. The coach of your current program may be able to recommend a club or a coach who would have the knowledge base needed to support your child in an inclusive setting.

SUMMING UP

The toughest thing for a new skater is figuring out where his or her body parts are in space once you add in this crazy, new, slippery surface! Once new skaters can learn to "quieten" their body and calm their movements, they have better control of their body and can make more purposeful movements to master some of the basic skating skills including gliding, stopping, hopping, twisting, and spinning. Take your time getting comfortable on the new skates and on the ice surface to encourage a positive first experience on the ice. Once a new skater can independently take several steps without falling, skating becomes much more enjoyable! For those skaters who become fluent in pushing and gliding, the feeling of the wind in your face as you smoothly move forward can be a very freeing and relaxing experience. We hope that your skater learns to love skating as much as we do!

RESOURCES

Examples of national skating organizations and learn to skate programs

Australia

Ice Skating Australia Incorporated, Aussie Skate
www.isa.org.au

Canada

Skate Canada, CanSkate
www.skatecanada.ca

United Kingdom

National Ice Skating Association of Great Britain, Skate UK – Learn to Ice Skate
www.iceskating.org.uk

United States

United States Figure Skating Association, Basic Skills Program
www.usfsa.org

Chapter 9

SWIMMING
Life Skills for the Water
Laura Dumas and Veronica Smith

WHAT'S GREAT ABOUT SWIMMING?

Where I grew up we were fortunate to be surrounded by cool mountain-fed lakes that despite their frigid temperature, became our swimming holes as soon as summer was officially announced! I have great memories of time at the lake, racing my sisters out to the diving wharf, basking in the sun (hopefully with a bit of sunscreen on, but I doubt it!), and getting my parents' attention before making a magnificent (in my mind at least!) swan dive off the board. Summer wouldn't be summer without a family picnic and a dip in the lake!

I became a pretty skilled swimmer over the course of my childhood, but I didn't learn how to do it all by myself. Like many other children my age, I took many lessons and practiced as often as I was able at the local pool. I was lucky, I learned to swim early and there were lots of supports to help me learn and lots of places to practice. For some children with ASD it isn't so simple. Learning to swim and to be safe around water environments is sometimes delayed. Often parents of children with ASD are hesitant to join swimming lessons because of their children's sensitivities, social, and communication challenges. There are many ways to support these challenges and we hope that we'll address many of them in this chapter.

Swim programs are available in countries all around the world (see "Resources" section at the end of the chapter). What's cool about swimming is that it's never too early or too late to start! Swim programs can begin as early as infancy with "Mom and Tot" programs. Beginner swim programs in many communities also extend into adulthood. In this chapter, we'll describe a swim program that was adapted to accommodate learners who need more support, and discuss a variety of strategies to help make a child's first exposure to water a safe, fun, and worthwhile experience.

BENEFITS OF SWIMMING

Swimming is a recreational activity that people have engaged in for centuries, in fact, ancient drawings found in Egypt depict people swimming as far back as 2500 BC! Not only does swimming have a long history, it also has many health benefits. For example, an hour of vigorous swimming burns up to 650 calories and works out all of the body's major muscles. The action of swimming is great for heart and lung health and is a demonstrated stress reducer. The warm environment of a pool can facilitate increased mobility, enhancing muscle tone and more efficient movement (American Red Cross, 2004). The water's buoyancy makes swimming an ideal exercise for those with stressed joints or muscles. As such, it also has therapeutic and rehabilitation benefits for those who need low-impact exercise. Swimming also has the potential to be a social activity. There are many organized activities that people enjoy throughout their lives such as competitive swimming (read Daniel's story in this chapter), synchronized swimming, water polo, scuba diving, and general fitness. Given all these benefits, swimming is a very popular and accessible recreational sport.

RESEARCH FINDINGS ON THE BENEFITS OF SWIMMING FOR CHILDREN WITH ASD

Of the sports reported on in this book, swimming probably has the most research associated with it. According to these studies, swimming is thought of as a good sport to engage in for children with ASD, and the benefits are not just about learning to swim! Early studies demonstrated that engaging in a swimming program was complementary to other forms of intervention geared at facilitating language development, adaptive behaviours, and independence (Bachrach et al., 1978; Best and Jones, 1972; Hamilton, 1972). More recent research indicates that children with ASD, even those with delayed communication skills, can learn to swim (Rogers, Hemmeter, and Wolery, 2010; Yilmaz et al., 2010), and demonstrate collateral benefits in social abilities (Pan, 2011). A study by Yilmaz et al. (2004) demonstrated that after a 10-week swimming program children with ASD demonstrated better balance, agility, muscle strength, and cardiovascular fitness. With these improved skills, children are able to enjoy family outings at pools, outdoor lakes, and oceans with increased opportunities for physical fitness and fun.

AN EXAMPLE OF AN ADAPTED LEARN TO SWIM PROGRAM: SWIMABILITIES

For two years, Laura Dumas has run SwimAbilities, a "learn to swim" program serving families of children and teens with special needs including ASD. Laura is an occupational therapist (OT) and Red Cross-certified water safety instructor. After years of working with children with ASD and other developmental disabilities, she knew that there were many children who needed more support to learn to swim and to understand the essential safety skills around water environments. She developed SwimAbilities to address some of these needs.

Who participates?

Children and teens (aged 3–16 years) with varying abilities and needs have participated in the SwimAbilities lessons. Groups include about 10 children at a time, all diagnosed with special needs, and occasionally include one or two siblings of the participants. An instructor facilitates the lessons, and a parent or volunteer is required to be in the water to provide individual support for each new swimmer. Due to the instructor's background as an OT, volunteers are recruited primarily from OT training programs at the university. Recently, the program was manualized in order to train some of the program's volunteers who hold Red Cross Swim Instructor certification. Currently, there are about half a dozen instructors who are trained in the SwimAbilities program.

Where and when do they swim?

Children swim once a week for 8–10 weeks per session. Sessions are 45 minutes long and take place at a local leisure centre with other group swim lessons. Siblings are invited to join the sessions and parents are invited to join in or watch from the bleachers depending on how comfortable their children are getting into the water.

What does the program look like and how does it help the children learn swimming skills?

The goal of the program is to increase water safety and swimming skills. Each 45-minute session includes 35 minutes of structured lesson time, with a slow pace and goals that are highly individualized and achievable. The last 10 minutes of the class is typically used to support the children who need time to transition out of the pool.

Table 9.1 Session breakdown and description

Program components	Description
Introduction (5 minutes)	Greetings, attendance, safe entries into the water, and an introduction song or activity (e.g. motor boat, get so wet! – children splash and move around the water)
Review (5 minutes)	A previously mastered skill is reviewed. This may include getting wet for level 1, blowing bubbles for level 2, floats for level 3, and warm up swims for level 4
Skill teaching (15 minutes)	The children's mastered skills are built upon and new skills are added and practiced
Safety or skill game (10 minutes)	A simple game focusing on either water safety or swim skills is played
Free time or transition time (10 minutes)	Children have time to play and practice the skills that they have learned over the session, or play a favorite short game or activity. Some children need the time to transition away from the pool

Why do we need alternative delivery methods such as SwimAbilities?

The SwimAbilities program parallels the Red Cross learn to swim program with a few important modifications: the skills are broken down into smaller steps and children are more closely supported by volunteers (see Table 9.1 for a description of the session content). Swimmers are provided with visual supports to help prepare them for class (see Figure 9.1). The new swimmers are grouped in one of four levels after their first session in the pool. The first level focuses on exposure to water and the initial basic skills. The second level works toward independence in the initial swimming skills, and the third and fourth levels work on increasing technique, distance, and provide an introduction to deep-water work. Throughout all the levels, the children and their families or aides are taught how to be safe in the water. Parents and caregivers are taught holds and techniques to support the new swimmers in learning new skills.

GETTING PREPARED TO GO SWIMMING FOR THE FIRST TIME

The first experience in a pool for any new swimmer (or a parent of a new swimmer) can feel overwhelming! Trying to sort out the new environment while adjusting to how the body feels while standing and moving in the water can be a lot to handle! However, there are a number of different ways to help a new swimmer prepare for his or her first experience. In this section, we'll describe some strategies to help your new swimmer cope with some of the new sensory experiences, describe different swimming attire, and introduce the basic skills to get you started.

STRATEGIES TO COPE WITH THE NEW SENSATIONS IN THE POOL

- *Hey, that feels weird!* The feeling of water on the body is unique and different from the temperature and pressure of the air. Take it slowly and try it out in small steps (sink, tub, backyard play pool).
- *It smells funny in here...* Most pools use chlorine to kill germs in the water but chlorine produces a distinct odour. Keep an eye out for pools that use additional methods to cleanse the water including ozone or ultraviolet light treatments. These methods can help reduce the smell of chlorine.

Figure 9.1 Swimming lesson visual support

DANIEL'S STORY

Susan McCann

As a family, we feel it is important to be involved in a variety of sporting programs. Our son Daniel has some of the fine and gross motor delays common to others with ASD. He also displays some of the social difficulties including limited eye contact and absorption in his own world regardless of the activities around him. This lack of attention makes coaching him somewhat challenging.

Like a lot of other families, we like to go on vacations that involve water sport opportunities. It was on one of these vacations that we realized our five-year-old son Daniel had no fear of the water – unfortunately he was not a good swimmer. As he became more interested in the water, we had more worries than fun on our holiday. Neither my husband nor I felt able to instruct Daniel to become a better swimmer and we were concerned about how Daniel would fare in a community swim lesson setting. When we returned home, we were thrilled to come across SwimAbilities, a community-based program that was geared for participants who need additional support to achieve beginning swimmer skills.

To prepare for our next vacation, Daniel started taking swimming lessons with Swimabilities. It was apparent that the extra and targeted attention he received in SwimAbilities had noticeable positive outcomes for his swimming techniques. Unfortunately, SwimAbilities did such a

terrific job of teaching Daniel that he was swimming at the upper level of the program by the time he completed his first session! His further practice on vacation moved him beyond the scope of that program, but that experience showed us that with extra support Daniel not only became a proficient swimmer, but also developed the necessary skills to be safe around water environments.

This summer, we asked Daniel if he would like to compete in "swim racing," and he agreed enthusiastically. This led to him joining a swim club. What better program for a child on the spectrum? This is a team sport where an individual's achievement can benefit the team if doing well, but doesn't really disadvantage the team if the individual is having an off day. The only adaptation the club made was

Photo 9.1 Daniel swimming

to require an aide to swim with him for daily practices and attend swim meets to help him get where he needed to be at the right times. Daniel has accomplished a lot in the swim club program. This past summer he competed in five swim meets, completing 17 individual races and placing as high as third place in a race. He also participated in a swim-a-thon where he swam 1150 metres in an hour. More importantly, he has made friends with several children in the club that are his age.

It's amazing the progress he has made in a single year – he just turned seven. Daniel is looking forward to competing in the swim club again next summer as well as enjoying the swimming opportunities on this winter's vacation.

Selecting a swim program

Our most important recommendation in finding a swimming program in your community is to check out whether the instructors are certified through a recognized instructor training program (e.g. Red Cross Water Safety Instructor Training). With a trained instructor, you are more likely to get instruction that promotes safety. A focus on safety can never be underestimated, knowing how to swim and behave safely around the water, quite frankly, can save your life.

To find out if there is a specialized program in your community for children with ASD or for those who need specialized support, start by contacting your local pool, and speak to the program director. These professionals can guide you to a program that can make special accommodations for your child or put the supports in place to provide the right kind of instruction with a trained instructor. You may need to be specific in outlining your child's characteristics to the program director or instructor. In Chapter 3 we provide some suggestions about ways to help them understand your child.

Equipment

Finding the "right" equipment is a fairly easy thing to do for swimming. Fortunately, there is very little equipment required. Below you will find both required and optional equipment, as well as a brief explanation of each. Recommendations from doctors regarding specialized equipment (such as ear plugs when a child has tubes in their ears) should always be followed.

Swimsuit

The best swimsuits fit well, and do not have any buoyant components such as foam inserts. Foam flotation inserts in swimsuits are not recommended because they change the child's balance and make it harder for them to swim independently and be safe in the water.

Some children with ASD who have touch and pressure sensitivities may prefer closer-fitting swimwear that provides consistent pressure and remains in place when worn. Others may prefer their swimwear to be somewhat loose to avoid the sensation of pressure against the skin. Alternatively, for swimmers who seek the sense of pressure on their skin or who get cold easily, full-piece body suits (that fit like a one-piece t-shirt and shorts) or tighter fitting swim shirts (aka rash guards) are good options. The term "rash guard" is borrowed from scuba diving and reflects the fact that it prevents the wearer from rashes caused by abrasions. In addition, these types of suits also protect the wearer from the sun so they are a good choice for outdoor swimming.

⚡**TIP** Full-piece swimsuits typically have a zipper in the back of the suit. For those swimmers who have difficulty keeping their swimsuits on, full-piece swimsuits can help prevent disrobing!

(a)   *(b)*

Photo 9.2 (a) Swimmer in bathing suit; (b) Swimmer in rash guard

For girls who like loose-fitting clothing, wearing a bigger size of swimsuit is a possibility but not recommended. Loose-fitting suits can change the way the body moves in the water and may fail to provide adequate privacy for the swimmer. Rather, it is preferable to choose a larger sized full-body swimsuit because it can provide more coverage and privacy for the swimmer.

For swimmers whose feet are sensitive to touch, wearing slip-proof sandals can provide a barrier between the deck and the participant's feet while walking on the bumpy, rough deck. While in the water, touch sensitivities can be addressed by wearing water shoes or water socks.

Swim diaper

Children who are not yet toilet trained for bowel movements are required to wear a swim diaper in the water. The swim diaper needs to be able to pass fluids through the material, but retain solids. As such, regular diapers or pull-ups are not suitable in the water. Swim diapers come in both disposable and reusable fabric forms. Disposable swim diapers are typically made up to a child's size large. Fabric swim diapers are available up to adult sizes. The larger sized swim diapers may need to be ordered online (see "Resources" section at the end of the chapter).

Goggles

Many swimmers prefer to swim with goggles because it keeps the water out of their eyes and allows them to clearly see obstacles while underwater. Goggles fit well when the eyepiece creates a firm suction action around the swimmer's eyes for two or more seconds without the strap to hold it in place. For those swimmers who find this suction action uncomfortable, swim masks are an option. However, note that swim masks reduce peripheral vision, which is necessary for safe swimming. As such, the use of swim goggles is preferred over swim masks.

Photo 9.3 Ian in face mask

Ear band/swimmer's wax/ear plugs

Ear bands, swimmer's wax, or ear plugs are seldom needed. However, for swimmers who find the feeling of water in their ears painful or find the noise in the pool overwhelming these supports are worth a try!

Swimming caps

These days, swimming caps are usually worn by people concerned with keeping their hair dry or not exposing it to pool chemicals. Most children find wearing swimming caps uncomfortable and are often reluctant to put them on. However, if your child objects to getting his hair wet, trying a swimming cap out might be a solution. Give it a go but be warned that putting it on your child's head is likely to involve lots of encouragement!

A WORD ABOUT FLOTATION DEVICES: SOME ARE USEFUL IN LEARNING TO SWIM AND OTHERS AREN'T

- *Personal floatation devices (PFDs): NO.* Personal flotation devices and lifejackets are not necessary to learn how to swim. PFDs change the child's centre of buoyancy making it harder to learn how to swim and move in the water independently.

- *Inflatable arm bands (i.e. water wings): NO.* These are also a no-no in swimming lessons. Although arm bands keep the arms and front body afloat, similar to PFDs, they do not allow new swimmers to learn to understand their own buoyancy and float independently.

- *Flutter boards and "noodles": YES!* Flutter boards and noodles (one-meter-long bendable foam floatation aid) that the new swimmer can hold on to are very useful for learning to swim. So why are these helpful, but PFDs and water wings are not? These objects are helpful for a couple of reasons:

  - a swimmer must hold onto these objects rather than wear them and

  - these objects can gradually be released as the swimmer becomes more confident in the water.

Caution: These types of "buoyancy aids" should never be used without supervision as they are not a replacement for an adult helper.

SO WHEN DO I NEED A PFD?

PFDs or lifejackets are required when on a boat. While they can be fun to use to explore deep water, they should never be used as a replacement for supervision. If the child is put into a PFD because they frequently run toward deep water, rather than wearing a PFD or lifejacket, behavioural intervention on stopping, waiting for permission to go into the water, and self-rescuing skills such as swimming to the edge should be explicitly taught to that child.

PREPARING FOR YOUR FIRST SWIMMING EXPERIENCE

Children with ASD do well in the water when they are comfortable and able to predict what is going to happen next. These swimmers often benefit from supports that link the steps that make up the goal. There are many ways to help prepare a new swimmer for the unique characteristics of the swim environment and the new setting: swim lessons. Let's take a look at a few ways you can help prepare your new swimmer.

Try on the equipment

Trying on your swimming gear prior to coming to the pool will save you time at the pool and give the new swimmer a chance to familiarize him- or herself with the feel of the swimsuit and other gear. The new swimmer might try getting familiar with the equipment in the tub or shower. This will help prepare the swimmer for the sensation of wearing wet clothes and alert you to any adaptations that you might need before getting to the pool.

Prepare for communication: Swim talk!

Becoming familiar with the language of swimming can prepare the new swimmer for the pool environment. Table 9.2 below provides some new vocabulary or "swim talk" that the new swimmer will encounter during lessons.

Table 9.2 Swim talk

Movements/ activities	Body parts	Equipment	The pool
Arm circles	Arms	Clothes	Deck
Back/front	Chin	Earplugs	Deep end
Blow bubbles	Ears	Flutter board	Help
Float	Face	Goggles	Pool
Glide	Feet	Noodle	Shallow end
Jump	Legs	Nose plug	Shower
Kick	Mouth	Swimsuit	
Splash	Nose	Towel	
Swim	Tummy		
Walk			

TIP If a student needs visual supports, you will need to waterproof your visuals. The following strategies are helpful for waterproofing: use a thicker laminating paper at a hotter setting, leave extra laminating around the outside of each picture, and only hole punch (if needed) the clear laminated edge rather than through the paper.

Getting wet

Make sure you take it easy the first time the new swimmer goes in the pool. Remember, a parent should always be prepared to get into the water for the first lesson. Begin by walking your child through a wading pool or a very shallow part of the pool such as a ramp or stairs, where his or her legs and feet can get used to the sensation of the water. As the new swimmer becomes more comfortable, gradually have him or her move into the water, from knee-high and thigh-high, to waist-, chest-, and shoulder-level, always ensuring that the new swimmer is consistently supervised and within arm's reach of an adult. Once the water level reaches the swimmer's arms, encourage arm movements through the water. These actions will help familiarize the swimmer with the sensation and resistance of the water.

Tour the pool

You will need to educate yourself about the facility where your swimmer's lessons take place. For example, some pools have leisure components such as "lazy rivers," slides, or waves. These components are distracting and are often accompanied by noises (e.g. loud alarms are sounded before waves start). Figure out what the new pool environment is all about before you take your new swimmer to tour the pool. You may need to sit on the pool deck for several sessions to get used to the activity and new sensory experiences. Make sure you explore the pool and change rooms with your child and, when possible, try to meet the instructor before the first lesson. For many new swimmers, instructions about safety are necessary before heading out onto the pool deck! Reminders to walk (not run) on the pool deck are very important.

Take a shower

Pools require their patrons to have a cleansing shower before going in the water. If your swimmer doesn't like showers (and many kids don't), avoid putting hand creams, lotions, or oils, or soaps on your child prior to going in the pool. You may wish to ask for special permission for your child not to have a shower before the lessons.

STRATEGIES FOR INTRODUCING WATER FOR THE FIRST TIME

- *Try the tub first.* Start small and try practicing being comfortable in the water in the tub. Try putting on the swimsuit to make it clear that you are practicing swimming. The use of the swimsuit not only helps your child get into the routine of getting ready for swimming, but can also provide a cue to distinguish *bath time* from *swim time*.

- *Bring on the toys!* Fun objects including diving weights can be used to encourage the swimmer to reach into the water. Diving weights are excellent for this purpose because they sink quickly to the bottom. They also come in a variety of sizes, colours, and shapes and are relatively inexpensive.

- *Start where it's warm.* Entering the pool after a shower can make for a very chilly surprise. Try the warmer pool first, or try wearing long-sleeved swimwear. Alternatively, you may also try to dip or wet your feet in the pool first, rather than putting your whole body in at once. Small splashes of water onto the legs or pouring water with fun toys can help give the body a chance to acclimatize to the water temperature.

- *Strategies for decreasing anxiety around water on the face.* Some individuals are particularly uncomfortable when it comes to getting their hair or face wet. Wearing a swimming cap and goggles is a useful option as it keeps the water out of the child's hair and eyes. It is important to remember to allow the swimmer to become used to the sensation of having water on their head and face *at their own pace*.

Initially, some swimmers might cover their face with their hands or a cloth to help to slow down the feeling of water coming down their face. To help transfer these skills to the pool context, you might introduce the swimmer to standing under a showerhead at the pool. Most facilities require patrons to have cleansing showers before entering the pool so practicing in the shower at the pool can take care of two steps in one!

YOUR FIRST EXPERIENCE: CHECKLIST

Do you have everything you need for your first day in the water? Look through the checklist below. Are you missing anything?

My swimming checklist

To do	Done!
Equipment check – swimsuit, swim diaper (if not yet toilet trained), goggles (if needed), and nose plug and/or ear band/swimming wax (if needed)	☐
Try out equipment at home and practice getting wet	☐
Explore the swimming pool and change rooms and take a shower	☐
Meet the swimming instructor	☐
Wait for the teacher or a parent to say it's okay to go in the water	☐
Now I'm ready to go swimming!	

BASIC SWIMMING SKILLS

Swimming programs are often broken up into age groups such as infant–toddler, preschool, and school-aged. Children who have little or no swimming experience and who are around the age of six will typically be placed in a swimming program that introduces them to basic swimming skills and water safety through games and fun activities.

Similar to other sports, swimming lessons are structured to introduce increasingly more complex skills as students master each level presented to them. Over time, the sequences of movements become longer, the physical demands (e.g. swimming distance) are increased, and the difficulty of the skills gradually increases. Now that your new swimmer has been introduced to the water, it's time to get cracking on the basic skills that will create the foundation for all other skills to follow (see Table 9.3). Let's check out these basic skills and how you might go about introducing each of these skills to a new swimmer.

Blowing bubbles

Blowing bubbles is the first swimming skill to learn. Blowing bubbles is important because it prevents swallowing or inhalation of the pool water. It also helps new swimmers learn how to regulate their breathing in the pool environment. As beginners learn to take longer to expel the air from their lungs, they increase their capacity to stay underwater longer, which allows them to practice the many strokes they need to learn to stay afloat. All in all, the goal is to have the swimmer blow bubbles consistently whenever they go underwater, so that when they come up, they are able to immediately take a breath.

Table 9.3 Basic swimming skills at a glance

Type of activity	Basic skill progression	Next steps
Blowing bubbles	Above water, exhale air through the mouth while making a noise (i.e. raspberries – these translate to bubbles when under water)	Same thing, now underwater. Next, encourage blowing bubbles through the nose
Going underwater	Face in the water – nose and eyes!	Underwater with the whole head!
Floating	Physically assisted front and back floats	Front and back floats with a buoyancy aid
Standing up from a front float	While floating, tuck knees up to the tummy	Scoop the water up to push the bum up and stand up
Gliding	From standing position, push off with feet, arms out, face in water	Add a kick!
Kicking	Hang on to the edge of the pool, face in water blowing bubbles and kick	Add kicking to the front and back float

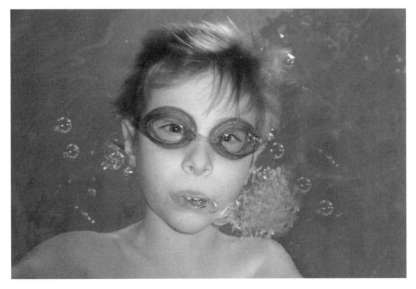

Photo 9.4 Blowing bubbles

Troubleshooting bubble blowing

Blowing bubbles can be a difficult skill to learn, especially if the swimmer has not learned how to consciously exhale through his or her mouth or nose. It can also be a scary skill for a beginner to perform if he or she has made the mistake of inhaling while underwater at a previous swim outing! For swimmers having difficulty blowing, try some of the activities listed below (Table 9.4), lots of beginners need practice learning to blow bubbles and it is best to make it fun!

Table 9.4 Bubble blowing strategies

Blowing the air	• Model blowing air out of the mouth – exaggerate! • Let the swimmer place his or her hand in front of your mouth to feel the movement of air, then coax him or her to try it him- or herself. Tip: The sensation of air is more pronounced when the student's hand is wet!
In front of the mirror	• Practicing blowing in front of a mirror! • Take turns steaming up the mirror!
Blowing with objects	Simple cause and effect activities also help develop the strength and control of blowing. • Blowing bubbles using different-sized wands. • Blowing at small feathers to keep them in the air. • Playing a game of table hockey by blowing ping-pong balls or pompoms (craft supply) across a surface (or on the water – they float!) and into the "goal." • Blow cotton balls by themselves, or by using straws.
Blowing in water	To help a beginner become comfortable with blowing bubbles into the water, a variety of focused activities can be used: • Blowing bubbles into water held in his or her hands. • Blowing bubbles in a bucket or another toy. • Blowing right into the water.
Getting your eyes wet while blowing	Blowing bubbles with eyes in the water is the next step. • Keep the eyes open and count the fingers! Hold up one to five fingers and encourage kids to count while blowing! • This can be done while at the pool, or even when in the bathtub. Tip: If the swimmer is significantly uncomfortable opening their eyes under water, goggles are a great option (see p.147 for more information on apparel).

Going underwater

New swimmers are often quite nervous about going underwater, but if they are supported in small steps, it is usually much less stressful. A slow progression of getting wet, splashing, putting parts of his or her face in the water (chin, lips, nose, cheeks, eyes, forehead, etc.), before going underwater can make going underwater much less threatening for a beginner!

:.Q:.**TIP** To help with going underwater, get some things that sink to the bottom of the pool and ask students to retrieve them. This non-structured game will help swimmers experiment with weight transfer in water as they bend forward in the water.

It is best if the new swimmer initiates putting his or her face in the water under his or her own power. If the student needs assistance, it is important that he or she be verbally prepared before any physical assistance is provided. For example, while facing the swimmer and holding his or her hands, the adult would say: "We are going to go underwater – one, two, three – blow bubbles!" Next, the adult would go underwater with the swimmer. *Underwater time should be two to three seconds total to ensure safe assisted submersions.*

:.Q:.**TIP** Water up the nose hurts a lot. After prompting to blow bubbles, if the adult holds the swimmer side by side in a front float position (see "Adult support and physical guidance" box for more information on physically assisting a new swimmer) and goes underwater in a forward or front swim motion (forehead first), water is less able to go up the nose.

ADULT SUPPORT AND PHYSICAL GUIDANCE

There are lots of ways that adults can provide support in the water, but unless the adult is a trained swim instructor, they should always take guidance from a trained coach. In general, support can be provided to a new swimmer by: (1) placing your hand under the swimmer's armpits; (2) holding his or her hands; or (3) supporting his or her tummy. Remember, when you are physically supporting a new swimmer, you are acting as the swimmer's buoyancy aid. To encourage independent swimming as soon as possible, replace your physical support with a buoyant object. Some examples of flotation objects include barbells, noodles, marshmallow sticks, and flutter boards. Once the swimmer is using a flotation object, this frees you up to model some basic skills!

Floating

As the swimmer gains proficiency in blowing bubbles and going underwater, working on floating is the next step. Some beginners, especially young children, spend a lot of time working on feeling comfortable floating. So how can you assist a new swimmer in learning how to float? Let's look at a few different strategies (see p.159 for examples). You'll notice that the photos depict a number of physical supports that you can use in the pool.

- *Front floats: Face to face.* This helps to provide reassurance and gives you an opportunity to model activites such as blowing bubbles.

- *Side-by-side holds* are also options for swimmers who are increasing their independence or need a little boost to progress to the next step.

- *Back floats: Under the armpits.* Start by holding the swimmer under his or her armpits, and having the swimmer rest his or her head on the adult's shoulder. Remember to keep the swimmer's ears out of the water.

- *Buoyant objects.* Replace the adult physical guidance with a buoyant object (e.g. flutter board).

Once the new swimmer can blow bubbles and float, it is time to combine these skills! Start by encouraging the swimmer to first put their eyes in the water and then blow and lift his or her feet off the ground. You can support the swimmer in lifting his or her feet by physically supporting the student, having the student hold the pool wall or lay on a floating mat.

Standing up from a front float

So now you're floating, how do you get down? Learning to get yourself upright from a float via trial and error often increases the anxiety around swimming since it's tough and the results are unpredictable. Standing up from a float includes a sequence of movements (see p.160 for examples). Let's try them out:

1. Bend knees in to tummy.

2. Scoop the water to push the bum down toward the bottom before standing up.

3. Push the feet toward the bottom of the pool and stand up!

Photo 9.5 Supporting floats

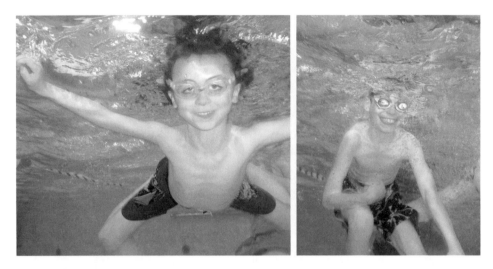

Photo 9.6 Standing up from a float

-ϙ-**TIP** Standing up from a float will help children learn about weight transfer in the water. As soon as kids can safely stand up from a float, swimming really takes off, so this is a very important skill.

Gliding

Gliding is the action of moving through the water either on the back side or on the front side of the body. The goal here is to get new swimmers to independently push off on the pool floor or wall and then glide for about three metres. Once the new swimmer can do this, he or she is usually ready to add in arm movements and kicking. However, learning to glide can involve a bit of sinking or at least the sensation of sinking, which is uncomfortable for many new swimmers! So how can we help support successful gliding?

- *Adult support.* Have an adult pull or push the child through the water while the swimmer holds onto a buoyant object.

- *Push off the wall.* One can initiate a glide by pushing off the wall or off the bottom of the pool.

-ϙ-**TIP** Use visual language that helps new swimmers learn about what gliding looks like. These might include a "pencil," "torpedo," or an "uncooked noodle."

💡**TIP** *Fading physical assistance.* Once the swimmer is comfortable going underwater (even if they are not yet starting or standing up on their own), it's time to pull back on our level of physical assistance while still ensuring a positive experience for the student. For example, the coach may help the swimmer go underwater as usual. Next, the coach gently pushes the swimmer underwater to another adult who is about 10–30cm away. For this 10–30cm, the student is briefly swimming independently (usually one to two seconds on the first few tries)!

Kicking

Once gliding is mastered, new swimmers can be introduced to kicking while holding on to the edge of the pool or holding a buoyant object. If kicking is learned at a young age (3 to 5) it tends to come quite naturally to most swimmers. If it's learned as an adult it's much harder.

💡**TIP** A good verbal cue for kicking is, "try to shake your feet off," this motion has them relaxing their feet, which is what has to happen to have an effective kick.

Good technique for kicking starts from the hip and progresses down a relaxed leg to the knees and through the ankles. The swimmer's knees should pass each other on every kick. Kicking can be practiced in the water or on land. Adults can help swimmers feel what their legs should be doing by having beginners hold the wall. From this position, the adult faces the swimmer's feet. Next, the adult can use his or her thumbs to gently keep the swimmer's knees from bending significantly while holding the front of the swimmer's knees with his or her fingers, helping the child to kick from his or her hips.

💡**TIP** Good kicks that come from the hip rather than the knees or ankles take a lot of practice! Many students begin to learn how to kick from their hips around the age of six or seven, but it often takes many more years of practice and instruction before the kicks are consistently made from the hips with full power.

WHEN CAN WE TRY MORE ADVANCED SWIMMING SKILLS?

This question is best answered by a certified swimming instructor who has watched the new swimmer while in the pool. Rely on your local coach to help your student advance his or her swimming skills. However, once a swimmer has mastered the basic skills presented in this chapter he or she should be able to independently swim on their front and back for three metres without touching the bottom of the pool. These skills should form a very solid base from which a student could enter lessons with his or her community peers of the same swimming ability. There are many swimming skills still to come but some of the next include adding kicks, arm movements that accompany recognized strokes, and safety skills for deep water.

SUMMING UP

Additional practice will be required for all new swimmers who have acquired the basic skills. Usually buoyancy aids are available for use during "public swim" sessions to obtain additional support when learning and performing a skill. Children also need a lot of time to play around in the water to get used to their bodies in this new environment. This can never be achieved during half-hour swim lessons. So, get out with your kids and have some fun in the water!

RESOURCES

Examples of learn to swim programs

Australia

AUSTSWIM
   www.austswim.com.au/welcome.aspx

Red Cross
   www.redcross.org.au

Swim Australia
   www.swimaustralia.org.au

Canada

Red Cross
   www.redcross.ca

YMCA
   www.ymca.ca

Swim For Life
   www.lifesaving.ca

United Kingdom

Amateur Swimming Association
   www.swimming.org/asa

Red Cross
   www.redcrossbritain

United States

American Red Cross
   www.redcross.org

YMCA
   www.ymca.net/about-us

Swim America
   www.swimamerica.org/Home.jsp?team=sa

United States Swim School Association
   www.usswimschools.org

ACKNOWLEDGMENT

In writing this chapter, Veronica would like to acknowledge the editorial guidance of Elizabeth Williams, Red Cross Instructor and Manager, Recreation and Culture for the City of Nanaimo, British Columbia.

Chapter 10

KICKING THE HABIT
Martial Arts Training for Families with Children with ASD
Jonathan Rivero and Stephanie Patterson

WHAT'S GREAT ABOUT MARTIAL ARTS?

After years of home martial arts "self-study" (mostly from imitating action movies with my dad and practicing on makeshift punch bags – rice sacks, coach cushions, and padded living room chairs), my mom finally enrolled me in a taekwondo class at the age of nine. At last I had an official outlet to show off my moves safely – I was in my element to say the least. It was a new beginning and way of life; training with a real Master was just like it was in the movies! Grand Master Sung Ju Kim and his teenage sons became my new mentors. Over the years, they demonstrated superhuman feats of leaping over people to break boards in the air, crushing multiple slabs of concrete with their hands, head, and feet, and winning hundreds of sparring matches at tournaments. I followed in their footsteps, winning multiple provincial and national championships in sparring and poomsae pattern competitions. The most important skill they taught me was not a specific kick, block, punch, or breaking technique, but the skill of striving to always do my very best in all of my endeavours. To many of my own students, I have become their role model. Twenty years later, my journey has led me to know a simple truth: the only true master that motivates, inspires, and teaches us is within ourselves. This is the indomitable spirit of martial arts.

WHAT ARE MARTIAL ARTS?

Originating in Asia, martial arts encompass a number of different practices including judo, karate, and taekwondo. Each of these traditions includes a unique set of techniques, philosophies, and styles of practice. For example, some forms of martial arts focus on physical outward expression, self-defense, and competition, while others focus on inward awareness, meditation, and personal growth.

Traditional martial arts emphasize elements of eastern philosophy including mediation, restraint, control, and the practicing of patterns (sequential movements against an imaginary opponent) (Twemlow et al., 2008). Through this type of instruction, one cultivates the core concepts of giving and receiving guidance, physical fitness, respect, patience, perseverance, honour, and a sense of personal responsibility (Fuller, 1988). Study of the impact of martial arts on students' psychological well-being indicate that as students progress in belt rank (colour denotes level of skill acquisition), they demonstrate increased self-esteem, self-confidence, adaptability, independence, and improved personal and social identity (e.g. Finkenberg, 1990; Kurian, Caterino, and Kulhavy, 1993).

TAEKWONDO

One example of a popular martial arts practice is taekwondo. Taekwondo will be used as the primary example and focus of this chapter. Translated as the "art of the foot and fist," taekwondo combines combat techniques, self-defense, exercise, meditation, philosophy, and sport. Taekwondo was founded in Korea and today, is one of the most practiced martial arts in the world. It is estimated that there are more than 60 million practitioners in 184 countries (British Taekwondo Control Board, 2011). In 1988, taekwondo was made an official Olympic sport at the 2000 Summer Olympic Games in Atlanta, Georgia.

As the sport has grown, national taekwondo associations have emerged around the world to facilitate the development of both recreational practitioners and elite competitors. These organizations also oversee the development and certification of taekwondo coaches as well as member clubs and schools. Now more than ever, martial arts training is popular among members of the general public including special populations such as individuals with physical challenges (parataekwondo – see Taekwondo Canada in "Resources" section for more information) and individuals with developmental disabilities.

Unlike other sports covered in this book, including swimming, skating, and tennis, taekwondo does not have a standardized flagship beginner program. Rather, taekwondo can be practiced in several forms. Although the fundamental skills are similar across practices, the curriculum, movements, and labels for those movements vary by school. As such, there are several governing bodies that oversee the development and standardization of their own practice including for example, the World Taekwondo Federation, International Taekwondo Federation, and United Taekwondo. The school of your choice may belong to any one of these different governing bodies (see "Resources" section at the end of the chapter for a list of associations by country).

Benefits of martial arts participation

There are many benefits to participating in Martial arts, not only for the individual with ASD but for the whole family. Martial arts provides opportunities for physical activity as well as learning strategies for self-regulation and self-control through fun routines and activities. It is a great way to practice motor co-ordination, planning, and strengthening skills and requires only an appropriate amount of open safe space. In martial arts practice a student learns what it feels like to have a quiet, still body and how to control his or her own movements. For individuals with ASD who often have difficulties with self-regulation and monitoring inner activity levels, martial arts may be one way to support an athlete's understanding and control of both a quiet body and a quiet mind.

This chapter touches on the general benefits of martial arts participation (specifically, taekwondo) and describes an adapted martial arts program for individuals with ASD and their families. In this chapter, we will: (1) provide an example of an adapted taekwondo program; (2) provide suggestions for choosing an appropriate program and school for your athlete and family; (3) learn how to use strategies to facilitate success prior to the first class; and (4) walk through the early fundamental skills. Through this example, you'll hear about an adapted taekwondo where students with ASD and their families have learned martial arts skills and learned to engage in self-regulation strategies.

AN EXAMPLE OF AN ADAPTED TAEKWONDO PROGRAM: THE YOUNG MASTER CLUB

- M – mental clarity
- A – always courteous
- S – self-regulation
- T – taekwondo
- E – expression of self
- R – respectfulness

What is the Young Master Club?

Based in Edmonton, Alberta, Canada, the Young Master Club is designed to teach families self-regulation and motor skills via adapted taekwondo. The program began in 2005 as a pilot project with five children with ASD and has since grown to include over 70 families.

Who participates?

Currently, the Young Master Club is a community program available to any family that is interested regardless of ability, experience, or the child's developmental level. Three classes are available based on the child's age (7 and under; 11 and under; 18 and under. Groups include participants with ASD, volunteer student coaches, rehabilitation medicine professionals, and an assistant instructor who is an adult diagnosed with Asperger's Syndrome and a 3rd Dan Blackbelt (which translates to a level 3 of 10 blackbelt levels). A vital component to the program is full family participation. Parents and other caregivers are strongly encouraged to attend the sessions and participate alongside their children. This family-level participation creates an environment where families can learn, have fun, and engage in sport together, and also helps give parents the skills necessary to help their children practice outside of the formal sessions.

What do the participants learn?

The Young Master Club has adapted typical taekwondo practice in multiple ways to support children with ASD. It includes a number of adapted movement sequences, adapted sparring, and a number of additional resources. For example, students are provided with videos of movement sequences at their level of ability to practice at home with their families. During class, students participate first in no contact sparring to learn to cope with the feelings associated with being kicked or punched without being touched. This form of sparring helps students develop the self-control needed to refrain from reacting aggressively and helps provide an idea of what sparring will be like once they begin contact sparring.

The Young Master Club Leadership Team

In 2010, the Young Master Club inducted its first leadership team with six of the most advanced students. The mandate of the Young Master Club Leadership Team is to develop leadership skills through coaching beginning participants and assisting the head instructor. Here's what one Young Master Leader had to say about his experience:

> What being a leader means to me is, being a good role model for the younger young masters and for the old young masters when times are challenging. I teach every young master to listen, think, look, not talk, and body still. I also practice those five rules in my spare time... Being a leader makes me feel happy and proud. (Young Master Chris, Leadership Team)

Young Master festival

Since 2008, the Young Master Club has hosted a festival that showcases families' abilities and skills through a public belt testing. The focus of the festival is family participation where children and parents compete in contact, individual sparring, team sparring, poomsae (movement patterns) including patterns that they have learned or created themselves, and finally, "habit board" breaking (see Benjamin's story in this chapter for a description).

Components of the taekwondo program

The taekwondo curriculum includes a number of different components including anaerobic and aerobic training, poomsae (set movements and pattern sequences), hosinsul (self-defense techniques), gyeorugi (contact sparring), relaxation exercises, throwing and/or falling movements, and special techniques for power activities (including the breaking of wood boards or bricks of concrete). In addition, taekwondo focuses on mental discipline, respect, self-control, courtesy, integrity, and etiquette.

Benefits of an adapted taekwondo program for children with ASD

The skills taught in a taekwondo program can be harnessed as tools to support individuals with ASD and other special needs in their everyday lives, while also providing an opportunity for participation in a fun, active sport. For example, the use of deep breathing techniques taught in taekwondo can be used as a daily practice for calming and self-regulation and incorporated into daily routines such as getting ready in the morning or doing homework. In the adapted taekwondo program, in order to be considered a Young Master, it means that you are constantly giving your all to be better than you were before. The coach, Jonathan Rivero puts it best, "I believe that if people do their best and give it their all in any sport, one day, they will truly master it in the best way that they can."

BENJAMIN'S STORY
Chris and Julie Davie

Our son Benjamin, is a bright eight-year-old who has exceptional talents in many areas. Autism has brought challenges for him and for our family in pursuing activities to keep his mind and body healthy. As a family, we were interested in pursuing opportunities for recreation and sport. We enrolled the whole family (Mom, Dad, Benjamin, and Sebastian) in taekwondo over two years ago. At the time, we thought that taekwondo might be out of our reach but we were pleased to find that the Young Master Club program included a number of strategies that helped everyone learn the skills.

Family participation meant that we all had to attend the group sessions and practice at home. We soon found that if we didn't pay attention and learn the moves during the session, we couldn't help Benjamin practice. So during our lessons everyone (parents and kids) learned the value of listening to the coach as well as the value of working as a team to ensure that "no one gets left behind"– our group motto.

One of the most important skills that we have taken away from taekwondo and applied at home is deep breathing as a strategy for calming down. We reference deep breathing in any situation where we feel anxiety is the culprit for challenging behaviours including homework time, at the dinner table, and when we are helping Benjamin end one activity and begin another. To our surprise, we are able to redirect Benjamin in his activities and continue to create a healthy environment at home – it works! On top of that, we actively practice other taekwondo skills including protective skills (blocking) and getting out of the way of danger; something children with autism are often challenged by.

Watching Benjamin succeed in taekwondo has been an emotional experience. One of the skills we learned was how to break a wooden board with our hands and feet. Before breaking the boards for the first time, we were a little nervous. Breaking the board is used to symbolize breaking old habits and achieving new goals. Each participant has to identify something in their life that they would like to improve and write it on the board. Benjamin picked his own goals starting with saying please and thank you, then moving on to home responsibilities including remembering to turn off the playroom light when he was done playing. As we watched Benjamin relentlessly attempt to break the board we were overwhelmed with pride to hear that board crack. Habit board breaking has consolidated the concept of goal setting for our family.

Engaging in taekwondo has positively affected our family dynamics, taught us life skills in working toward being your best, and reinforced the importance of goal setting. We have seen Benjamin grow in his taekwondo abilities. It has been emotional to see him work alongside us diligently to master the kicking patterns and earn new belts. He proudly counts in Korean, puts up his hand to answer questions, and has even volunteered to teach others how to perform a skill. If you asked us a year ago if Benjamin would be capable of this, we would have politely dismissed the notion. Practicing taekwondo has allowed us to see our son in a new way.

Photo 10.1 Instructor Jon Rivero with students Benjamin and Sebastian (left to right)

GETTING PREPARED TO TAKE ON MARTIAL ARTS FOR THE FIRST TIME

Selecting a martial arts program and preparing to participate

There are several preliminary steps that you can take in order to be prepared for your first martial arts experience. Let's explore these steps:

1. Set your intentions

Try to decide as a family what you want to get out of participating in a martial arts program. Keep in mind that throughout your participation, these goals may grow and change. For some families, participation itself is the focus, while for others it could be gaining fitness, self-control, respect, discipline, and/or self-regulation. Whatever your intentions are, be clear and write them down. Take your written goals with you as you explore potential martial art studios and talk about them with your potential instructors. Focus your search on finding the right fit for your family.

2. Choose a martial arts studio in your community

Choosing a program in your community means choosing both a form of martial arts and a particular studio or school. A school that will provide a program that your entire family can enjoy together has many benefits including opportunities for parent modelling, family participation, and leisure enjoyment. Families that learn together can also grow closer together. Be sure to check out the options, visit websites, and read about the philosophies of each school because they can vary. For example, some schools might be more focused on competition, while others might be focused on inclusive participation and personal growth. Simply choose a school that fits your goals and values best. Determine what is important to your family and keep this in mind when selecting your school.

3. Talk with the head instructor and observe the class

Selecting the right instructor for your martial arts experience is one of the most important steps to success in any program. Ask as many questions as you see fit with respect to the needs of your child – especially around discipline (it can vary by school but push-ups, for example, are a common consequence for undesired behaviour). Do you need to make some adaptations to make the program work for your family? Is the school open to these kinds of adaptations or have alternative suggestions? Simply observing a typical class can give you a lot of information about the expectations and setting (see Chapter 3 for some suggestions on observing a coach). If the instructor and their assistants seem open to your feedback and the program seems to resonate with your philosophy on learning, then the likelihood of a right fit for your family increases.

4. Don't overthink it

A primary principle in martial arts is the concept of intuition and feeling. If it feels right to you and your family then do not overthink it. Don't get caught up in "paralysis by analysis!" This is the notion that procrastinating or simply not acting on your gut feeling, keeps you from participating.

5. Prepare to practice at home

Observing beginner classes can give you the opportunity to spot skills that your student will be covering in their first classes. Try practicing some of these skills at home before arriving at your first lesson. There may also be time before or after the class to ask any questions that were not answered in the class, or to ask for extra help in breaking down a skill to practice at home with your athlete. Consistent practice between classes will help your student to learn, remember, and develop the skills and techniques that are taught in class each week. Don't worry if you think your student can't do what the other kids in the class are doing. Martial arts is an individual journey of discovery, you just might find out more about your child than you know.

6. Adapting equipment for home

Equipment used as targets for hand or foot strikes can be adapted for use at home. Try substituting the pads for old pillows or cushions. Practice only if it is conducted in safe space with adult supervision. This type of family participation at home may enhance enjoyment and provide motivation despite the challenging nature of the skill. Remember to consult your instructor if you have questions about how to break down a move or sequence so that practicing at home can further develop skills in between classes.

7. Kick the habit

If fear of participating in a sport or activity for your new athlete with ASD has prevented you from participating in the past, "kick" that habit, trust your intuition, and simply choose to participate in what you feel is the right program for your family. There is a Buddhist proverb that says: "The master appears when the student is ready." Decide to be ready.

STRATEGIES FOR SUCCESS IN THE DOJANG

- *Does the dobok (training uniform) feel too scratchy?* Try washing it several times to soften the material or wear a soft shirt underneath to reduce rubbing.
- *Belt too rough on the tummy?* Try tying it multiple times to help soften the belt.
- *Is the kihap (yelling) too loud?* Try a studio with noise-absorbing properties (e.g. dance studio) or noise-cancelling headphones.
- *Uncomfortable in bare feet?* Try socks with grips on the bottom or water shoes with your instructor's permission.

OTHER CONSIDERATIONS FOR YOUR FIRST MARTIAL ARTS CLASS

Although taekwondo is an active sport, it also heavily emphasizes quiet breathing, control, and inner focus. Learning to silence one's mind and body can be challenging for anyone and may be a novel experience, especially for younger children. Although these new expectations may be challenging at first, there are a number of things that you can do to help prepare a new student for his or her first experience.

Etiquette in the studio: Expectations

It is very important to understand the etiquette, routine, and base expectations of a martial arts school. Collaborate with your instructor to gain an understanding of what should be practiced prior to the first class. For example, some schools might want your family to be able to follow basic one- or two-step instructions prior to coming to class. If you are unable to speak directly with the instructor try checking out other available resources such as the program's website or student handbook. These resources may describe the expectations for class and the appropriate behaviour. Creating social stories and visual schedules with pictures that represent etiquette, commands, routines, and rules that can be reviewed a few times prior to the first class can also enhance familiarity and performance.

It is also important to speak to your instructor about the methods and philosophy of that particular school. For example, traditional martial arts programs incorporate military style routines that hold respect and conformity as staple values. These values can lead to specific and strict expectations for conduct during lesson time that include etiquette, routines, and rituals. Although these expectations can be challenging, with careful consideration of the choice of program and the supports put in place for the individual, you can help to foster successful participation in martial arts.

Check out the dojang: The taekwondo studio

Try heading down to the taekwondo studio to get a feel for the new environment. With the instructor's permission, get a feel for the dojang (e.g. walk on the floor mats, check out the mirrors, touch the bricks, check out other equipment) and meet your new instructor as well. The instructor may also be able to provide you with an introduction to some of the language that will be used during the group so that you can prepare appropriately.

Check out the dobok: Taekwondo attire

As part of your class, you will likely be asked to wear a "dobok." This refers to the belted white robe that is worn during taekwondo practice. The dobok is kind of like a v-necked poncho that slides over the participant's head and is pulled in at the waist by a belt. Your chosen school will likely make available a dobok for you to purchase because often each school has their own identifying uniform. If this is the case, you may be able to try on a dobok and/or purchase one. Take your new uniform home and practice wearing it around the house to get used to the feel and weight of the new robes and belt.

Talking the talk in the studio

Create a taekwondo vocabulary list to ensure that you have the necessary language available for participation in a beginner class (see Table 10.1 for a list of taekwondo terms). Since taekwondo was developed in Korea, a number of the commands and moves have both English and Korean labels. Be sure to write down the basic commands in the language that will be used during the program. In introductory taekwondo, important words include labels for movements and equipment. It may also be useful to take pictures to represent that command or action. Practicing the language and skills at home can help to familiarize your family with the commands prior to your first class. For individuals who use alternative and augmentative communication (AAC) including speech output devices (e.g. iPod touch, iPads, dynavox, etc.), be sure to synch your pictures to these devices so they are available during the class.

Try out being still and breathing

One of the key components of taekwondo is your breath. Taekwondo emphasizes the use of breath with movement, so developing some awareness of one's breath is very helpful. Before arriving at taekwondo, try practicing being still and counting or noticing your breath. Try this while seated first. Start by sitting still for two to five seconds at a time. Then, focus in on the breath. Try practicing four-second breaths: breathe in for two seconds and then breathe out for two seconds. Over time, your goal is to have breaths that are controlled and even, coming in and out through the nose. We'll talk more about breathing and strategies for breathing in the basic skills section to come.

Table 10.1 Taekwondo talk

Movement/ skill term	Activities	Korean words	Body parts	Environment
Attention	Be still	Dobok (training uniform)	Arm	Bricks
Bend	Circle time	Dojang (studio for practice)	Fist	Dojang (studio)
Block	Go	Gyeorugi (contact sparring)	Foot	Mats
Bow	Line up	Hosinsul (self-defense techniques)	Hand	Warm up area
Deep breath	Sit	Kihap (expression when you break a board)	Leg	
Horse riding stance	Stop	Joonbi (ready position)		
Kick	Warm up	Poomsae (movement sequence)		

WHAT TO DO WHEN YOU ARRIVE AT THE DOJANG

There are several strategies that you can use to help ease your new student into the lesson time.

Dress at home and arrive 15 minutes early
By getting your student dressed at home, you avoid potential line-ups at the dressing room and lessen the number of things that need to be done once you are in the dojang. Arriving dressed and with 15 minutes to spare will give some time for the student to adjust to the new surroundings.

Move and stretch, practice your breathing
Many taekwondo studios will have a separate area designed for warm up and stretching. Take a few minutes to have the student move around and warm up before the class gets started. This is also a good opportunity to practice your deep breathing and get the student prepared to use these skills in the class.

Relax and stay positive!
It's easy for both students and their families to become anxious while waiting to get started. Try to remember that this is an experience designed for fun and learning. Let your student see your excitement, stay positive and relax!

YOUR FIRST EXPERIENCE: CHECKLIST

Do you have everything you need for your first day in the dojang? Look through the checklist below, is there anything you're missing?

My taekwondo checklist

To do	Done!
Equipment check – taekwondo attire: dobok and belt	❏
Review taekwondo talk – if your athlete uses an augmented system (e.g. picture symbols, device) bring them along	❏
Reinforcers for great work	❏
Take off shoes	❏
Explore the room and meet the coach	❏
Warm up – stretch and practice your breathing	❏

TIP Keep in mind the three Cs when practicing your taekwondo skills: CLEAR (instruction), CONCISE (focus on one skill at a time), and CONSISTENT (repetition or practice).

BASIC TAEKWONDO SKILLS

Taekwondo practice involves many series of movements that grow in complexity and length as students progress through levels of mastery. The fundamental skill that you will be introduced to in this chapter represents the constellation of movements required to execute a "joonbi" or ready position (see Table 10.2 below for the list of skills). This is an essential movement in taekwondo because it is the way every movement sequence begins in taekwondo. As a student progresses, he or she will be evaluated via a sequence of movements or "poomsae." Joonbi is the first position in every poomsae. Poomsae increase in complexity and length as the student grows and develops. Once students have mastered a particular level of poomsae or movement sequence, they receive a coloured belt representing that level of mastery (solid colours and stripes). For students working on their first belt, the fundamental skills that will create the foundation of their taekwondo practice, the joonbi, are included below.

Table 10.2 Basic skills required for the first level of taekwondo mastery

Type of movement	Basic or introductory skills	Next steps
Being still	Sit still for two seconds	Stand still for ten+ seconds
Deep breathing	Lie down on back, place hands on tummy, and breathe in through nose, out through mouth	Rhythmic even breaths in (two seconds long) and out (two seconds long) of the nose
Making fists	Hold palms up with fingers splayed	From the open palm, fold the four fingers into the palm and then wrap the thumb across the fingers to make a fist
Training stance	Stand straight with feet together, elbows pressed into the sides of the body and chin tucked under (see skills section below)	Horse riding stance (see below for description)
Bowing	Stand in attention stance and look toward the toes	Smooth controlled bend at waist to a 90-degree angle
Ready (joonbi)	Mastery of the following basic skills: attention, bow, and make fist	Full ready (joonbi) sequence (see "ready-joonbi" description below)
Kick	Balance on one straight leg from basic stance	Hold one leg in the air to form a 90-degree angle with the body – hold for two+ seconds

Being still: Your first step in your taekwondo journey

Taekwondo practice requires a student to learn about what it feels like to have a quiet, still body and how to control your body's movements. Learning to keep still can be a battle for anyone, especially for children. The new student may have already been introduced to practicing being still. Let's review: (1) sit still for two to five seconds, and once successful; (2) move to standing still for two to five seconds. Slowly but surely, try to increase the time that the student is still up to a desired ten seconds and beyond.

TIP Once the student is standing still for five to ten seconds you are nearly in the attention position. To master the attention position, ensure that the student has his or her feet together and arms alongside the body. Now you're in the attention position, the student has mastered his or her first skill!

Deep breathing

Now that you have practiced having a still and quiet body, deep breathing is introduced. Breath for taekwondo comes in and out through the *nose*. You are looking to achieve *even breaths* where *the time to breathe in (e.g. two seconds) is the same as the time to breathe out (two seconds)*. Later on, the breath becomes linked to the actions you take with your body. Much like yoga, the body's actions will occur in sequence with a breath in or a breath out, creating a rhythmic practice.

:💡: **TIP** Since breathing through your nose can be a tough action to demonstrate with a clear visual cue, if a student is having difficulty understanding the concept, try breathing in and out through your mouth.

:💡: **TIP** Other visual aids can be used for breathing. Try a paper bag. Show the student the bag placed over your mouth. As you breathe in, the bag will collapse and as you breathe out, the bag will inflate. This creates a visual demonstration of the moving air. *However, please use CAUTION when working with any bag because it is a potential safety hazard for less experienced students and young children.*

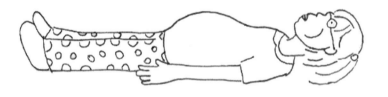

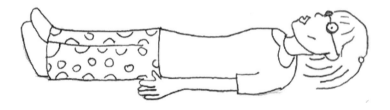

Figure 10.1 Rise and fall of belly

TIP Another visual for breathing involves watching one's belly move in and out. Have the student lie on his or her back and prop the head up with a pillow. Then have the student practice breathing in and out while watching his or her abdomen rise and fall with each breath. This same visual cue can be used with a model. Watching the abdomen rise and fall on another person as that person inhales and exhales can also act as a visual cue for the rhythm and timing of the inhale and the exhale.

Making fists

Creating a fist is an important first step for teaching a student how to block, strike a target, and focus attention in ready stance. A fist in taekwondo has one very important component: *the thumb sits on the outside of the fist*, NOT wrapped within the fingers. The first instinct of many new students is to put their thumb into their palm first, under their fingers. This can be detrimental later on, when the student is asked to put weight and pressure on their fists. When the thumb is wrapped inside the fist, this pressure can lead to dislocations of the thumb and other damage to the hand. So, it's very important for a student's health and safety to ensure proper placement of the thumb early on.

TIP To help put the thumb in the correct place, start with the fingers spread open like you would when someone says "give me five." Then show the student with your hands how only the four fingers bend into the palm of the hand while the thumb sticks out like a hitchhiker. Last, fold the thumb in on top of the fingers. This will help emphasize that the thumb is the last component of the hand to fold into the fist.

Photo 10.2 Ben's fists

Training stance

As you progress into taekwondo you will be introduced to a number of different body *"stances"* or ways of positioning your body. The first stance you will learn is the basic stance. By standing up straight you've nearly got it! Once standing straight:

1. Make sure your feet are together.

2. Tuck your chin in.

3. Bend your elbows so that your upper arms are tucked alongside your body and your hands are raised in front of your face.

Photo 10.3 Training stance

☀ **TIP** The following verbal cue may help as a reminder of the sequence of body movements when practicing training stance: "fists, chin, elbows in!"

Horse riding stance

Once the student has mastered this basic stance, the next stance is the *horse riding stance*. For this stance:

1. Move your feet apart so they are hip-width distance apart next.

2. Bend your knees.

3. Pull your elbows alongside your body and make fists.

The idea of the horse riding stance is to teach the student to brace him- or herself while standing. This stance is about balance. Ideally, in this stance, someone could bump into you and you wouldn't topple over! Keep working on this stance until you achieve this level of balance and stability (see Photo 10.4).

Photo 10.4 Horse riding stance

Bowing

Now that you are practicing standing still in the attention position, you can add another movement to this sequence: the bow. The bow is very important in taekwondo because it demonstrates that you have respect for your opponent (an important aspect of class etiquette). To get started, stand in the attention position. Next, tilt your head to look at your toes. With a straight, tall back, slowly bend at the waist to look at your toes. Stop bending once you create a 90-degree angle between your straight legs and your bent upper body.

TIP So how do I create a 90-degree angle with my body? If we think about standing straight and tall and then bending at the waist, a 90-degree angle feels like you are laying your tummy on a table while your legs stay very straight.

TIP To help new practitioners learn the rhythm of the bow, try adding a short phrase like "one, two, look at your shoe and up." This may help give a sense of the rhythm and length of the movement as well as the pause at the bottom of the bow.

Photo 10.5 Bowing

Ready (joonbi)

Mastering all of the skills above has now prepared you for taking on ready stance (or "joonbi" in Korean). Ready stance becomes very important to a taekwondo practice because it is the starting point for all of the sequences of movement that the student will learn. There are a number of steps in this sequence, let's take it one step at a time:

1. Stand in "attention" position.

2. Bow.

3. As you inhale, step your left foot out to the side so that your feet are hip-width apart.

4. With your arms straight, slowly bring your hands inward across your body with your palms up until your fingertips touch.

5. Begin to bend your elbows and draw your hands up to your collar bone.

6. Flip your palms over so that they face the ground and make fists.

7. As you exhale, begin to straighten your arms by pressing your palms down toward the floor.

(a)   (b)   (c)

Photo 10.6 Joonbi step sequence

Kick

Taekwondo involves many kicks. Key to learning to kick is mastering the balance and control necessary to execute even a basic kick. To start, practice balancing for two to five seconds on one straight leg with the other leg slightly raised in the air (see Photo 10.7). Once the student has mastered this, try extending the leg that is off the ground out in front at a 90-degree angle.

💡**TIP** Practice standing on one leg for two to five seconds at a time. This will help with balance transfer from the kicking leg to supporting leg. Feel free to make a game out of how long you can stand on one leg for. Do not forget to practice on both legs.

Photo 10.7 Balance for kicking

WHEN CAN WE TRY MORE ADVANCED TAEKWONDO SKILLS?

Mastering the basic skills presented in this chapter improves the student's ability to attend to instructions for the more complex skills and sequences of skills that are yet to come. For safety reasons, it is also important that taekwondo students can demonstrate that they know when it is and is not appropriate to use their taekwondo skills (in class and not on the playground). Once students have mastered the ability to control themselves by standing still for 10–15 seconds, follow basic directions, and balance on one leg for 10–15 seconds, they may be physically and mentally ready for more advanced skills. Some of the next skills that your student will learn include patterns of movements and a variety of kicks.

The poomsae

Learning to sequence motor movements is one component of taekwondo that can be challenging. However, taking on this challenge through taekwondo provides opportunities to practice and improve sequencing motor skills. Once you have mastered the fundamental basic skills, you will be engaging in "poomsae" or skill patterns that are core to taekwondo. This built-in repetition through practicing poomsae can help students learn to remember and sequence movements.

SUMMING UP

Of the sports featured in this book, the different forms of martial arts provide a unique focus on the practice of both mental and physical control and stillness. Taekwondo, for example, presents one avenue for students to learn about how to physically "be" in their bodies and to exercise thoughtful control of one's actions. Students can learn at their own pace and actively participate in a fun and physical activity while interacting with members of this new community. Good luck breaking those boards, kihap!

RESOURCES

Examples of national taekwondo organizations following World Taekwondo Federation Curriculum

Taekwondo Australia
   www.taekwondoaustralia.org.au

Taekwondo Canada
   www.wtfcanada.com

The British Taekwondo Control Board (BTCB)
   www.britishtaekwondo.org.uk

USA Taekwondo
   http://usa-taekwondo.us

Chapter 11

TENNIS
The Perfect Match

Shafali Spurling Jeste, Richard Spurling, and Stephanie Patterson

WHAT'S GREAT ABOUT TENNIS?

Tennis has been played for centuries with early illustrations and records of tennis type games in the early 12th century (Gillmeister, 1997). Today, countries all over the world have national tennis organizations, many of which have programs specifically designed to help introduce children to tennis as early as the preschool years (see "Resources" section at the end of the chapter for a list of national organizations and their learn to play tennis programs).

Each player has his or her own story to tell about how tennis is enjoyable and appealing for them. For one of the co-authors of this chapter, Richard Spurling, a love of tennis developed very early at just five years old. I was lucky to have started tennis at such a young age. By the time I was ten it was my favorite thing to do. I loved everything about the sport – I dreamed of being John McEnroe! I wanted to wear the same tennis shorts, shirt, shoes, and even the socks. When I played with my friends we tried to imitate his strokes and copied his serve. We would imagine we were in the final of Wimbledon and one of us would pretend to be Lendl while the other was McEnroe. Looking back now at that time in my life, I enjoyed the independence that I had – I could cycle to the tennis club and play tennis with my friends. When I was 15 I started to play more tournaments and enjoyed the challenge of being out on the court alone trying to figure out a way to beat my opponent. Being the best tennis player in my school gave me a lot of confidence and it was a great way to make a lot of friends. Even today, tennis continues to bring people into my life. Through my work, no matter where I live, whether it is teaching tennis at a club or running ACEing Autism, tennis is the constant variable in my life that opens doors to opportunities and people.

Tennis can be played anywhere, at any time. With just a racquet and a ball, you can enjoy tennis at many levels from spontaneous play in the yard, to recreational games on the community courts, or more competitive matches in organized leagues. No matter what level you would like to play there is a way to be involved in tennis. Importantly, with the advent of new programs and equipment designed with kids' size and abilities in mind, the opportunities for physically and developmentally appropriate tennis play are increasing. For many players, tennis can provide an avenue to participate in lifelong recreation and make connections with other community members in the process.

STRATEGIES FOR SUCCESS ON THE COURT

- *That feels weird!* Both the fuzzy ball and the grip of the racquet can feel odd. Try gloves to put a barrier between the player's hand and the equipment.
- *Are you playing outdoors or indoors?* Keep in mind the environmental conditions in two different styles of court (e.g. echoing indoors and sunlight and outside noises outdoors).
- *Crumbly bits are fun to play with!* Keep in mind that outdoor courts are often made from clay that can crumble and create fun places to dig or play that can distract a student from the task at hand: learning to play tennis!

In this chapter you will read about ACEing Autism, an adapted tennis program designed for children with ASD. The ACEing Autism program was developed by the husband-and-wife team of Richard Spurling and Dr Shafali Jeste in Boston, Massachusetts, USA, and now runs out of Boston, MA and Los Angeles, California. The experience of one participant will be highlighted and a number of strategies and supports that are used in ACEing Autism to facilitate players' learning will be discussed throughout this chapter.

AN EXAMPLE OF AN ADAPTED TENNIS PROGRAM: ACEING AUTISM

ACEing Autism is an adapted tennis program developed for children with ASD and other developmental disabilities. The program is designed to include players of all levels but typically takes in children and teens with little to no experience with a ball and racquet to help them gain basic tennis skills as well as the skills necessary to begin to navigate the game of tennis.

Who participates?

The ACEing Autism program began in 2008 and has served over 120 families of children with ASD, with many families participating for several years. Since expanding to Los Angeles, the program has served another two dozen families.

A key factor in the success of the ACEing Autism program is the dedication of the volunteers who donate their time on and off the court. Volunteers work one to one with children in the group, allowing parents the opportunity to both watch their children participate and to connect with other parents in the ASD community. Additionally, and invaluably, several parents of children who have participated in the program serve as board members and have helped to develop a program manual to support the delivery of the program in other tennis clubs around the country.

Where and when do they play?

The ACEing Autism program began in Boston, MA, and grew to include sessions at two local indoor tennis facilities: one using full-size courts and the other using child-sized courts based upon the United States Tennis Association's (USTA) Quickstart initiative. When arriving in Los Angeles in 2010, Shafali and Richard started a west coast ACEing Autism site. In Los Angeles the program is run in collaboration with the University of California Los Angeles (UCLA) Adaptive Recreation Programs on outdoor courts located on the university campus, and is currently expanding to include new sites within the city. At both sites, participants are grouped based on age and skill level. Younger children and new players are grouped together while more advanced teenage players take part in a separate session. Participants play for 50 minutes once a week.

What do the players learn?

ACEing Autism is designed to help children of all ages and abilities learn basic ball and racquet skills. Programming is individualized to fit each participant based on their prior tennis experience, developmental level, and motor abilities. The goal of the program is to help facilitate the development of racquet skills and techniques that are developmentally appropriate for the participant, which can range from balance and hand–eye co-ordination through to rallies with peers on the full tennis court.

Why do we need alternative delivery methods?

ACEing Autism makes use of a number of supports including visual supports, smaller courts and nets, and adapted equipment. In addition, further structure is built into this program to create predictable steps and routines helping children to understand what is being expected of them and what might be coming next. Each session is run with the same basic structure including a warm up followed by ball and racquet drills and then the introduction of new skills, followed by closing activities and games (see description below in Table 11.1).

Table 11.1 Session breakdown and description

Program components	Description
Warm up (10 minutes)	For example, running warm ups (e.g. high knees), ball and racquet warm ups (e.g. walking the dog – pushing the ball along the ground with the head of the racquet)
Tennis readiness skills (15 minutes)	Includes basic skills covered in this chapter including volleys, forehands, backhands, and more as the students master the skills presented
Drills (10 minutes)	Drill time focuses on one particular stroke. Sessions are broken down into two week-long blocks with each block focusing on a different stroke
Closing Games (15 minutes)	Fun group games: For example, red light green light, jail break, tag games

The objective of ACEing Autism is to offer sports instruction and service to families that have children with ASD. Shafali and Richard realized there were not enough play-based programs in the area for children on the spectrum. Through ACEing Autism players are not only learning tennis but they are improving motor skills, hand–eye co-ordination, social skills, and health. To get in touch with ACEing Autism staff, check out the contact information listed at the end of the chapter.

Photo 11.1 ACEing Autism group shot

ZOE'S STORY

Mira Tamir Spiegel

My daughter Zoe was just four years old when she took her first swing at tennis through Richard and Shafali's ACEing Autism tennis program for children with ASD. She has participated in the program since its inception and three years later she is still learning new skills. Now seven years old, Zoe is a very active, happy, and affectionate kid, but she definitely struggles with language, impulsivity, and social expectations. One of Zoe's relative areas of strength is athletics. She is extremely well co-ordinated and great at climbing, jumping, and bike riding. She also participates in horseback riding, swimming, track, and gymnastics.

Photo 11.2 Zoe

Zoe and tennis

Since Zoe was diagnosed with ASD five years ago, our lives have been so busy with autism-related therapies and interventions that we nearly forgot that there could actually be opportunities for fun and recreation for our family. Then we met Shafali and Richard and came upon what would become the ACEing Autism program. Tennis appealed to us for many reasons. I played competitively in college, my husband and I have always played recreationally, and our family of four seemed like a doubles game in the making. Next, there was Zoe's natural athletic ability. We thought she should have the opportunity to capitalize on her strengths and we realized that if Zoe could someday learn to understand the associated expectations, sports might be one of her best mainstream chances. Finally, what we really loved about tennis is that it is a social game with a natural "give and take rhythm" that requires a player to respond to the moves of the other player. We were hopeful that all the skills that a variety of teachers and therapists spent all week isolating and working on with Zoe could be practiced and reinforced in one tennis session.

Achievements and challenges

ACEing Autism has led to positive benefits for our whole family. In addition to learning some tennis, Zoe has benefited from the "social recreation setting" of the program and has also made great gains in her ability to focus and attend on the court. We have met a number of other families of children with ASD who we may not have connected with otherwise. Zoe's brother has met more kids like himself – typical siblings of children with ASD. While Zoe is out on the court, her younger brother is running around playing tag in the viewing area with other kids who know what it's like to have a sibling with ASD. We get the chance to interact with the program volunteers, to share with them some of the joys and challenges of raising a child with ASD, and those already studying or working in the field of autism share with us what they are learning. We've watched while college-aged volunteers have changed their majors or career plans because the time they have spent at ACEing Autism has made them realize what they want to do with their lives. We love knowing that we are helping to shape a future generation who will have the skills and the desire to understand people who have ASD.

Zoe continues to enjoy athletics and is making strides in her focus, attention, and engagement in tennis. ACEing Autism helps Zoe gain experience and skills in both the social realm and the athletic domain, while still having fun.

GETTING PREPARED TO PLAY TENNIS
FOR THE FIRST TIME

Selecting a structured tennis program... Or not...

How you support a new player during their first tennis experience will depend on whether or not you are accessing a formal program or if you are trying it out on your own. If you are participating in a structured program, you may be asked to come out onto the court with your player to participate in the program, while other programs may have the student participate independently or with the help of volunteers or other staff. Check with your player's coach to see what the expectations for family participation and assistance may be.

HOW DO I HELP MY NEW PLAYER LEARN THESE SKILLS?

If you are introducing tennis on your own, of course we want your experience to be a fun one that will motivate the student to try this again! Making the physical connection between the ball and the racquet and seeing the ball make it over the net is important to developing an understanding of the purpose of the game and how the game can be fun! But how do you do this? The primary method of support for a new player in their first attempts is to physically help the new player complete the new actions. The tennis swing has a number of steps in a fast-paced sequence. To physically assist a child, place your hand over the player's hand on the racquet and help him or her make the swing motion. Next, add the ball. In the same manner, help the player create the swing motion but, this time, make contact with the ball. This early bit of physical assistance will help the individual learn to make the appropriate movement and increase the frequency of successful connections with the ball. You'll learn more about strategies to help a student learn to swing the racquet later on in the chapter under "Basic tennis skills."

Equipment

Tennis is a great sport to try because you don't need much equipment to get out there and get started! The key types of equipment that a player needs in order to be comfortable and safe on the tennis court are as follows.

Clothing

Choose clothing that allows for movement, too tight or too baggy just won't do. Shoes fit for running are also needed. Please check with the program that you are enrolling in to see if tennis shoes are required. Tennis shoes can have additional benefits for the player because they provide more support for the heel and ankle than the average running shoe.

Balls and racquets

If you are not playing with an organized program that provides equipment, you will also need a ball and a racquet. When selecting a ball, consider low-pressure balls that bounce more slowly, these are easier for beginners to hit. Racquets come in a variety of sizes, with the smallest being 19 inches in length (48.3cm). This size of racquet is appropriate for a four-year-old child. Racquets increase in size in 2-inch (5.1cm) increments. As a player grows and develops more physical strength, larger racquets can be introduced. Consult your coach if you are unsure which size of racquet is appropriate for your player. Sports equipment store personnel can give advice on size. Some programs provide the type of equipment that is ideal for children to learn the game (e.g. child-sized racquets, low-pressure balls).

Other things

If you are playing on an outdoor court, consider light clothing, sunscreen, and lots of water to keep your player happy and healthy on the court.

TIP Many learn to play tennis programs for young players will make use of modified courts to help new players get into the swing of things as well as avoid injury from strain. The United States Tennis Association (USTA) learn to play tennis programs use smaller, shorter child-sized courts often called "zip zones." These smaller courts require less power from the player to get the ball over the net.

Supports to bring along

For a new participant, the tennis court may be a novel environment filled with many new experiences and sensations. While this may be exciting and fun for some players, others may find a number of these aspects challenging. For those areas that might be challenging, there are steps you can take to make for the best possible first experience on the court.

Photo 11.3 Zip zones/smaller courts from ACEing Autism

Visual supports

Keep in mind that many adapted programs have visual supports that fit within the structure of the program. However, if a student has specific visual strategies that are effective in other settings such as home or school then it may be helpful to bring these visuals along to the tennis court and apply them there (for more information on visual supports see Chapter 5).

Motivators

Sometimes we need a little extra motivation to get through challenging experiences. If you think that your player might need some extra support to keep motivated through the session, it may be helpful to bring along reinforcers such as special toys for break time, special treats, etc. However, please check with your tennis pro about policies regarding food before bringing edibles out onto the court.

Tennis talk

Like many sports, tennis includes a number of different vocabulary terms that children may not have otherwise come across in their day-to-day lives. Introducing some of the terms can help a new player prepare before arriving at the court. If the player uses an alternative communication system (e.g. picture exchange communication system) or an augmentative device (e.g. speech output device), then the appropriate symbols must be prepared so that the player can use language during the tennis sessions. The table below (Table 11.2) provides some examples of tennis vocabulary.

Table 11.2 Tennis talk

Movements/ tennis terms	Activities	Equipment/court	Other symbols
Groundstroke	Balance	Ball	Break
Backhand	Drills	Baseline	Hi
Forehand	Games	Court	Help
Volley	Warm up	Doubles alley	More
Serve	Racquet ready	Net	Toilet
Swing	Obstacle course	Racquet	Water
Ready position		Service line	
Follow-through			

Watch some tennis examples

For a beginning tennis player, it can be difficult to wrap your head around how the basic ball skills fit into the act of playing a game of tennis. What's the point of learning these skills and doing these drills? Watching tennis matches on television or clips on YouTube can provide visual examples of what real tennis games look like and help create a vision or goal while working on basic ball skills. For children or teens, watching other children or teens play a game really well may be more effective than watching adults play the game. Of course, adults will play well! But watching kids both play well and make mistakes can be a valuable teaching tool.

Increasing success with early ball skills

Some new players have a fear of balls and this can make tennis an anxiety-provoking experience. Many people are afraid of balls primarily because they are fast moving, unpredictable, and can cause pain if they hit you. Sometimes switching from a ball to an object that the player knows is soft (e.g. stuffed animal, larger/lighter ball, beach ball, balloon) may lessen the fear. These alternative balls may help the player develop the motor co-ordination and visual skill needed to hit them. As the student becomes more proficient at catching, throwing, or hitting these balls and objects, he or she may progress to balls and objects of various sizes and shapes that travel at different speeds, distances, and directions.

Ball and racquet experience

One of the first things that a new player will need to do before engaging in the game of tennis is get some experience with the ball and racquet. Playing simple activities with balls (e.g. roll the ball back and forth, assisting the child in throwing and catching a ball) can be a great way to get started! Tennis balls are relatively small and can be tough for little hands to catch and throw. You may try starting with larger balls (beach balls) and then progress toward tennis balls.

The tennis swing itself has a number of steps that can make it a challenge to learn. To introduce the body motion required for the swing there are four things that you can do at home to prepare:

- *Try the motion with a ball in hand.* As a starting place, have the player hold a tennis ball in his or her hand and make the swing motion. As the student swings his or her arm through, have him or her lightly throw the ball. This will introduce the movement and could be part of a catch type game.

- *Try a "hand racquet."* A "hand racquet" is a piece of equipment that is kind of like a mitten. The fabric mitten slides over the player's hand and can be used similarly to the first step where you make the swing motion with the mitt on your hand. In addition, you can add a foam ball to hit as you make the swing with your hand racquet.

- *Now try with a racquet.* Once you're comfortable with the first two steps, it may be time to add in the actual racquet. The racquet will have a different weight and feel to the ball or the mitten.

- *Try it in the mirror.* If you find yourself in need of additional visual cues during your practice, try the skills in front of a mirror at home.

Check out the court

If transitioning to new environments is a challenge for your child, it may be helpful to take some time to explore the tennis court. Taking a visit or two to the facility before the first session can help ease the transition to a lesson on the first day of class. This will allow for more peaceful exploration, give you a chance to talk about what the class will be like, and try out a couple of ball skills on the court. If it is not possible to visit the facility prior to your first lesson, check to see if the program/facility has a website. Images from the website can be used to help prepare the student before arriving on site.

Meet your pro and look over the schedule

By coming a bit early to the first session, you may also have time to take a few minutes for your player to be introduced to the tennis pro(s) as well as any volunteers or extra helpers participating in the program. If you are participating in an organized program, there will be the time to quickly go over the class schedule. What will the first class look like? Some programs may have visual or written schedules for the student to follow.

BASIC TENNIS SKILLS

Although tennis might seem easy enough on first glance, there are many sequences of movements and skills that go into the basic actions of tennis, especially the tennis swings. Moving quickly on your feet, anticipating how fast and where the ball is going, as well as deciding how best to return the ball, are all part of playing a successful game of tennis. But how do you get there?

Tennis can be a challenging sport because it involves not only controlling the movements of your body, but also learning how to manipulate the equipment. Below in Table 11.3, you'll find a quick reference list of these basic skills and their next steps, each of which we'll discuss in more depth in this section. We will focus on introducing the proper way to hold a tennis racquet, how a player should hold his or her body to swing, as well as how to effectively swing and make contact with the ball. You'll also find "tips" or teaching strategies for each of these components throughout this section. For a player who is new to tennis, these key skills and actions need to be mastered before he or she can progress toward engaging in a tennis "game."

YOUR FIRST EXPERIENCE: CHECKLIST

Do you have everything you need for your first day on the court? Look through the checklist below, is there anything you're missing?

My tennis checklist

To do	Done!
Equipment check – comfy clothes, runners, racquet and ball Outdoor court equipment check: hat, light clothes, sunscreen, water	❑
Supports – communication, visual, rewards for great work	❑
Sensory items for on the court – sunglasses, gloves, noise busters, etc	❑
Practice basic ball and racquet skills	❑
Explore the tennis court	❑ ❑
Meet the coach	❑
Warm up	❑

Now I am ready to practice my skills on the court!

Table 11.3 Basic tennis skills at a glance

Type of skill or movement	Basic skill	Next steps
Grip racquet	Hold racquet with appropriate grip for stroke being performed	Hold racquet with proper grip while balancing ball on racquet or dragging ball on ground
Ready position	Stand with toes facing the net, knees slightly bent and racquet in front pointing slightly to the ground	Try moving in and out of ready position quickly from different positions
Sideways body position	Standing facing forward, take your right foot and point it to the right	Move from standing facing the net to sideways position
Contact point	Identify where the contact point is	Move racquet into contact zone
Tennis strokes		
Forehand swing	Make swing motion while physically assisted	Make swing motion independently; then assisted swing motion toward ball on tee stand

Backhand swing	Make swing motion while physically assisted	Make swing motion independently; then assisted swing motion toward ball on tee stand
Volley	Give a "high five" to a stationary ball (start sharp straight action of the volley)	Stand at the net, have the player "high five" a ball that is fed to him or her

Grip racquet: Learning to hold the racquet

Tennis involves two main pieces of equipment: a ball and a racquet. One of the first steps in the journey toward learning to engage in a game of tennis is to understand how your body and these two pieces of equipment move together in space. How a player holds his or her racquet is an important part of his or her success in making effective contact with the ball. As players learn different strokes, they will learn the racquet grips that accompany these strokes.[*]

To help a player learn to hold the racquet, put the racquet in his or her hand and yours (hand over hand) and model the position for the proper grip. This can provide both a visual of the grip and help the new player adjust to the feeling of holding the handle and the weight of the racquet in his or her hand.

TIP There are several ways to try to facilitate the appropriate racquet grip, One of the simplest may be by "introducing the racquet" to the child. Hold the racquet out with the handle facing the child and ask the child to shake the racquet's hand. This should automatically produce the continental grip without extra technical language. This strategy could be used with or without any language. You might also try having the child grab the racquet like he or she is "holding a hammer."

---

[*]   Note that there are many different racquet grips that vary depending on the type of swing you are doing. These are fairly advanced skills so these changing grips will not be discussed in this chapter.

Photo 11.4 Correct racquet grip

Ready position: Getting ready to take on the ball

Now that you've got a firm grip on the racquet, it's time to move your body into a position where you have the best chance to successfully make contact with the ball. Imagine you are on a tennis court, facing the net and the player across the net. If you are right handed, turn your body to the right until you are sideways facing the ball (for left-handed players, turn to the left). Now your feet are facing an imaginary three o'clock rather than the net and your opponent. Think of stacking all of your joints on top of one another so that your knees are over your ankles, hips over your knees, and your shoulders are over your hips. Your knees are slightly bent and your feet are shoulder-width apart.

> **TIP** Imagine that the end of your tennis racquet is a "flashlight." Have the player imagine that the butt cap of the racquet is a flashlight and that they must point the flashlight at the person feeding the ball, or even at the ball approaching the racquet before they swing. Have the player stand sideways, holding the racquet ready to start the forward motion of the swing. We want the butt cap of the racquet or "flashlight" to point toward the net.

Sideways body position

The ready position is quite easily turned into the sideways body position. Have the player stand facing the net as they would for ready position. Then have the player taker his or her right foot and point it to the right (to three o'clock). This will naturally open the body to the side. Note that your left foot is still facing the net. So last, have the player pivot the heel of the left foot and point the toe to the right as well.

Contact point: Where the racquet meets the ball

Understanding the contact point on the racquet requires a player to start to develop an understanding of where his or her body, their racquet, and the ball are in space. Where should the racquet be? How high should the ball be when you hit it? These are all important components to understand in order to hit the ball! We want the racquet to make contact with the ball at knee height out in front of the player. For a right-handed player, stand first with knees bent. Then move the left knee to point in the direction of ball. In this stance, you are ready to move into the incoming ball.

TIP Gauging the contact zone between the player's hips and knees while both the player and ball are in motion is really hard! After the player has an understanding of where the contact zone is, begin by keeping both the player and ball still. For example, you can place the ball on a tee and then position the player next to the tee. This way, the player can gain a sense of where his or her body, racquet, and the ball are in space.

Photo 11.5 Tee ball

The tennis swing

There are multiple types of swings that you will use in tennis. However, for the beginner, there are three primary types of swings that you will learn including the: (1) forehand groundstroke, (2) backhand groundstroke, and (3) volley. Each of these swings requires different body positions and grip of the racquet. Let's take a look at each of these three types of swings.

Swing: Forehand groundstroke

The section on the "contact point" has moved us into the idea of now swinging the racquet to make contact with the ball. Although it may appear simple at first glance, there are a number of steps in the sequence required to swing and successfully hit the ball. Keep in mind that the racquet grip, sideways body position, and understanding of the contact point are the requisite skills for the racquet swing.

> ☼ **TIP** It may also help to practice holding the racquet while facing a mirror to help provide a visual of the ready position and the positioning of the racquet in relation to the child's body.

It is important that the player develops an understanding of the motion of the swing. Key to learning the tennis swing is putting the focus on creating a smooth controlled motion. The goal of a tennis swing is NOT to hit the ball as hard as you can. This is very different from other ball sports! There are three key concepts to learning a basic forehand swing. Let's take this one step at a time:

1. THE START OF THE SWING: HEIGHT

Where does the tennis swing start? Contrary to what we might assume, a tennis swing does not start as far back as you can stretch your arm but rather, your swinging arm is slightly bent. Imagine that while you are turning your shoulders to turn sideways your racquet is making a loop. The highest point of the loop is at shoulder height. As your hand drops your racquet continues its loop. The loop continues to the point where the butt cap of the racquet points to the approaching ball.

For very young children who may lack the strength to produce a full swing motion, you might begin to introduce the swing motion much lower so that the racquet is in front of the child. For younger children they must learn the groundstrokes from a sideways position. Have the child start his or her swing with hands next to hips with the butt cap point to the ball. The contact point is between the knee and hip and out in front.

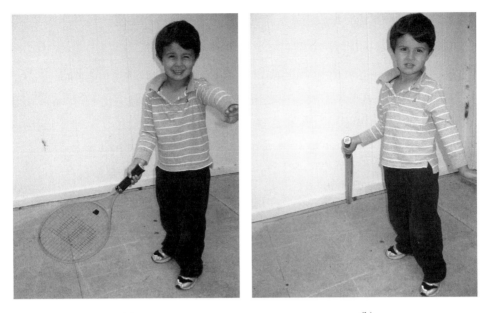

(a) *(b)*

(c)

Photo 11.6 Swing series

2. FLUID TRANSFER OF WEIGHT FROM START TO FINISH

Crucial to the tennis swing is the shift or follow-through of weight from the back leg through in the direction of the ball. Let's break it down:

(a) start with feet together

(b) step into ball

(c) swing as your right hip and shoulder move forward into ball

(d) try to "track" or follow the direction of the ball with the free arm that is not holding the racquet

(e) step into the shot so that you are leaning into the ball at impact.

3. SMOOTH AND SLOW MOTION

The motion of the swing is like a pendulum. The racquet swings through like a pendulum from "low" to following through to "high" at the end of the swing. Control of this motion is key in the tennis swing. A controlled motion will help make the transfer from the beginning of the swing motion to the finish. Let's imagine this movement. The start of the swing motion is where the player pulls his or her wrist and racquet back so that the end of the racquet is facing forward in the direction of the swing. Now from this position, the forward part of the swing begins with the shoulder and hip coming forward. The racquet extends out to the ball and the relaxed follow-through finishes over the opposite shoulder.

Photo 11.7 Swing finishing in backpack

Understanding where to point and direct the racquet at each stage of the swing can be difficult due to the quick pace of the motion in real time. A common error that beginner tennis players make is that they do not follow-through on the swing. The term "follow-through" refers to the end of the swing movement with the racquet moving back toward the player turning the base of the racquet handle or butt of the handle to face the net. The end of the tennis swing can be described as ending with the racquet in the player's "backpack" to emphasize the direction and the length of the movement.

TIP "Shadowing" or modelling the swing movement by hand-over-hand helping the player to move through the swing motion and the appropriate position can help them to visualize the swing and start to build muscle memory around the action of the swing movement. The tee stand can also be used to help a new player learn the motion of the swing. The player can begin to learn the feel of hitting the ball in the contact zone in the proper body position without having to adjust for a moving target.

Swing: Backhand groundstroke

The sequence of steps to completing a backhand swing is the same as the forehand swing but on the opposite side of the body. However, the movement of the backhand swing is often easier for new players because it is typically introduced using a two-handed grip. The movement also tends to feel more natural because the player's body and in particular, the player's shoulders naturally rotate into this shot. To have a successful backhand swing, a player must realize that the non-dominant arm is swinging the racquet. So, for a right-handed player the left hand is gripping the racquet tighter than the right. Then to swing, the left arm is the one propelling the swing of the racquet while the right arm gets a free ride!

TIP In similar fashion to the forehand swing, in a backhand swing follow-through is important! To help the student understand the full range of the backhand swing motion, have the student imagine the racquet finishing in his or her backpack.

Volley

A volley is the third type of stroke that a new player will likely be introduced to. The volley is unlike the forehand and backhand groundstrokes in four important ways:

- There is NO SWING in the volley stroke.

- Unlike a groundstroke, in a volley, the ball does not bounce on the ground before it is hit.

- This is because a volley takes place close to the front of the net.

- A volley is a short, compact, punch at the ball that requires a quick reaction during a tennis point.

Even though a volley seems very different from a groundstroke, it is similar in that you need to transfer your weight from back to front in a similar way.

Photo 11.8 Volley

Since there is no swing in a volley you can think of this action as a "volley with your legs." The force for this movement comes from the movement of your weight into the oncoming ball, NOT from the swing of the racquet.

> 💡 **TIP** For players that have limited strength and experience you can begin to learn a volley by holding the racquet by sides of frame (as though you could hold up the racquet strings as a mask over your face). Just like giving a high five to the ball, move the racquet straight forward with a firm grip to punch the ball. You can think of this like you are blocking the ball rather than swinging at it.

WHEN CAN WE TRY MORE ADVANCED TENNIS SKILLS?

Up to this point, we have included skills and exercises where both the player and the ball are stationary. The addition of a ball in motion can make the skills much more challenging because the player needs to learn how to track a moving ball in space and then co-ordinate the timing of his or her own actions with the ball in motion. This leads to a fairly complex set of steps including steps for the grip, body positioning, and swing sequence that must now be linked to the moving ball. It can take a new player a fairly long time to master the swing motion and stationary exercises. However, if the player appears to have mastered the stationary exercises, you may want to try out a moving ball as a next step. The simplest way to introduce the moving ball is by having a second individual gently feed the ball from a short distance away to the player who is standing in position and who may also have an adult to physically guide the action for the first few attempts.

SUMMING UP

Once your new player has developed an understanding of how to navigate his or her body alongside a racquet and ball, you're well on your way to a game of tennis! There are many different ways to play tennis (as well as other racquet sports) – you can play alone and as part of a team or group. Try experimenting with different settings and different types of racquet play to see what works best for your player to get into the game!

RESOURCES

Examples of National Tennis Organizations and Learn to Play Tennis programs

Tennis Australia, Tennis Hot Shots (age 5–12)
www.tennis.com.au

Tennis Professional Association (Tennis Canada), Progressive Tennis (age 5–10) – FUNdamentals curriculum
www.tenniscanada.com

British Tennis: Lawn Tennis Association (LTA), Mini Tennis (age 4–10)
www.lta.org.uk

United States Tennis Association (USTA), Quick Start Tennis (ages 10 and under)
www.usta.com

ACEing Autism contact information

To find out more about the ACEing Autism program please contact Richard Spurling at aceingautism@gmail.com, or check out the website: www. aceingautism.com. You can follow us on Twitter and like us on Facebook. You can also view videos of the program on www.youtube.com.

ACKNOWLEDGMENT

Richard, Shafali and Stephanie would like to thank Harvey Rubin for his dedicated work with ACEing Autism and for the many photos contributed to this chapter.

Chapter 12

SOCCER
Join the Soccer Team!
Veronica Smith

WHAT'S GREAT ABOUT SOCCER?

Although this completely gives away my age, in the small community where I grew up, they only had soccer leagues for boys! My sisters and I would go and watch our big brother play on Saturday afternoons. While standing on the sidelines, all I could think about was how much I would like to "get into the game." By the time I was in college, soccer leagues for girls were popping up all over the place and I joined a team with my younger sister, Jane. Truth be told, I was a pretty crummy player but loved going out for practices, getting some exercise while figuring out how to handle the ball, and socializing with my teammates. When it came to the competitive games, I was more of a cheerleader than a goal scorer – I was better at directing the other players to pass the ball rather than taking a turn myself! My younger sister Jane was a pretty talented player, so I would frequently yell, "Pass it to Jane, pass it to Jane" even if I was more optimally positioned to take the ball! Regardless, I came to love soccer and have been thrilled to find that it has become one of the most inclusive team sports around. These days, not only are girls included in soccer but there are co-ed teams and, most importantly, teams for kids who need extra supports. In this chapter, we profile two such special leagues – a unique indoor soccer program for kids with ASD and an outdoor league that includes all children (and their siblings) with any sort of special need. We interviewed several of the enthusiastic individuals associated with these programs to develop the strategies and skills featured in this chapter, and we're excited to share it with you here.

HISTORY OF SOCCER

Soccer, or "football" as everyone but North Americans know it, has been described as the most popular sport in the world. The game has been around in some form for thousands of years, so we have few clues about who invented it or in which country it originated. The Chinese people are acknowledged to have the earliest known version of the game where in 1697 BC, a Chinese emperor invented "tsu-chu," a game played with the feet and a leather ball (Lewis and Lalas, 2000). Other early variations of the game were played in Greece, Rome, South America, and some Pacific Islands but the modern form of soccer originated in England in 1863. At that time, there were many variations of the game, so in order to create a common standard, "The laws of the game" were written and subsequently sanctioned by the London Football Association. These laws, or rules, are still used and guide the form of the game that is played today (US Soccer Federation, 2000).

SO WHY SOCCER?

Soccer is the only team sport featured in this book. We chose it above others because it is one of the easiest team sports to learn. It is also inexpensive to play and is available in most communities – big or small. In many countries, soccer can be played year round (whether that be indoors or outdoors) and it is easy to pick up and organize (see "Resources" section at the end of the chapter for a list of soccer organizations across countries). Soccer is also a game that you can learn to play at any age, kids can play as young as four or five, and many soccer enthusiasts play the game their whole life (or as long as their knees hold out!). Size doesn't matter either! Big and small players are seen on even the pro teams. Despite the age, size, or level of expertise, all players are working toward combining skill, speed, and an understanding of the rules to get good at the game.

A GREAT "FIRST" TEAM SPORT

Thankfully, the object of soccer is relatively simple: score more goals than the opposing team by getting the ball past a goalkeeper and into the net. In many ways, the simplicity of soccer makes it the perfect "first" team sport for athletes with ASD. Learning to play with and to pay attention to others is a challenge for many players with ASD, so the less complicated the game, the better! But the skills learned in soccer also provide repeated opportunities to work on many needed abilities. For example, a core skill in soccer is the ability to pass the ball to others. To learn to pass the ball you need to exercise basic attentional skills including paying attention to the ball and your teammates, as well as skills to appropriately get the attention of others. In addition, playing a game of soccer requires that you understand your role on the team and work together with your team on a common goal (literally!). Paying attention and working with others are important needed skills for people with ASD and one of the great collateral benefits from participating in this sport.

Did I mention fun? Even though it requires effort, playing soccer and being part of a club or team provides a wonderful sense of belonging – for parents and kids, alike. This is important for anyone but especially important for kids, young adults, and adults with ASD.

STRATEGIES FOR SUCCESS ON THE SOCCER FIELD

- *Pitter patter of feet!* During indoor soccer, sounds can echo in the gym. This can be irritating to sensitive ears. Quiet break rooms and noise-cancelling headphones provide a couple of good options for quiet time.
- *It's too hot!* Or maybe too cold? Outdoor soccer leaves players privy to the ever-changing elements of the outdoors. Make sure you have the appropriate equipment (e.g. sunscreen and light clothes or jackets and mitts) to make for a pleasant and safe experience.
- *So much going on!* There's lots to look at on the soccer field including the other players, spectators, balls, and nets! Visual supports such as coloured pinnies to identify teams and other visual cues can help players sort out the visual noise on the field.

A SOCCER PROGRAM FOR CHILDREN AND EARLY TEENS WITH ASD: I CAN PLAY SOCCER

The Canucks Autism Network (CAN) is an organization that was founded in 2008 in Vancouver, British Columbia by Paolo and Clara Aquilini. In 1996, their son received a diagnosis of autism. A decade later the Aquilinis are advocates for people with autism, with a commitment to improve community options available for children and teens. They started CAN, a foundation associated with a National Hockey League Team, to create opportunities for children with ASD to participate in community sports. As part of this effort, CAN developed the "I CAN Sports Series." I CAN Play Soccer is one of these programs.

In the I CAN Play Soccer program, sport-specific skill development is not the only objective. The program also aims to encourage general physical and social development. This is achieved in two ways: (1) by providing an environment that supports the individual needs of the athletes, and (2) by delivering instruction at a pace that accommodates the learning styles associated with ASD.

Who participates?

Over the past three years, 90 families of children with ASD aged 5 to 15 years have participated in I CAN Play Soccer programs. The programs have been conducted in 11 communities around British Columbia. Any child with ASD up to the age of 15 years can join and no prior soccer knowledge is necessary. For safety reasons, the children are grouped by age (5–11 year olds together and 10–15 year olds together). This grouping prevents accidents based on body size and strength. Each group has an experienced soccer coach who has viewed a training DVD from CAN. In addition, there are several trained volunteers and paid one-to-one workers who support the kids during practice. Ideally, there are 10 kids in each group. Yet, the groups have become so popular that group size can be up to 15 children to avoid wait listing participants. Siblings are invited to join in and parents are encouraged to socialize with other parents on the sidelines or just take a rest while watching their children participate.

CAN has done a superb job of figuring out what it takes to create and support their program in new communities.[*] Each I CAN soccer program is resourced with a training manual and DVD, a program manual, a visual schedule and appropriate symbols, a bag of low bounce soccer balls, several collapsible nets, some cones and discs for drills, name tags, and coach and volunteer t-shirts.

Where and when do they play soccer?

Soccer practices are usually held in the afternoon or early evening for one hour during the week or on the weekend. The children meet once a week for a 13-week session. The practices are usually held indoors in school gymnasiums or community centres. Indoor venues mean that the practices can be conducted year round and that children do not require special footwear or clothing, just comfortable indoor shoes that they can run around in are all that's needed!

---

[*] The CAN centre currently only has funding and the mandate to support programs in the province of British Columbia, Canada.

What do the students learn?

The program focuses on the following fundamental soccer skills: dribbling, passing, kicking, and shooting. Most activities are conducted as a group to build a team atmosphere and a sense of community. The focus of the activities is on team bonding, listening skills, following directions, taking turns, and building potential leadership skills.

What does the program look like and how did it help the participants learn soccer skills?

It is clearly established at the first practice and onwards that the coach is the person to listen to for all instructions: transitions, new activities, and drill details. A visual schedule is often used to introduce and close each activity. The start and end of each activity is clearly marked by the coach using cues including "first," "then," "next," and "after" (see example on p.214). Each week, the children can expect a predictable routine – starting with "free time with the soccer ball" and followed by "team activities" interspersed with frequent breaks. To maximize player attention, the coach strategically gives clear, simple verbal instructions while the players are seated on the floor. The instructions are intentionally kept short, to just two to three minutes per activity – so that the children can experience maximum practice time. In addition to the visual schedule, the coach sometimes uses an erasable white board to show the players how to move around the room or where to stand in relation to each other or the props that are sometimes used for drills. Skills and drills become incrementally more challenging over the 13-week sessions as the children progress and older children (who have been involved in more than one session) may participate in a scrimmage at the end of each practice. See Table 12.1 for a description of a typical lesson.

Why do we need alternative delivery methods like I CAN Play Soccer?

The structure of league-based community soccer programs is often challenging for many kids with ASD, moving at too quick a pace and lacking enough repeated practice to learn each individual skill. In the I CAN program, the focus is on creating a sense of community where children feel safe to practice skills repeatedly and parents feel confident that additional learning supports will be provided for their children to have fun and not be left more stressed and discouraged by participating.

Photo 12.1 Visual schedule

Table 12.1 A typical I CAN Play Soccer lesson

Program components	Description
Free time (5–10 minutes)	• Coach welcomes the group • Volunteers encourage the players to warm up by playing with soccer balls (e.g. dribbling, passing, kicking) allowing for transition into the gym
Team meeting (5 minutes)	• Coach calls players over to the "team meeting" spot and invites them to sit on the floor announcing that, "Free time with the soccer ball is over" • Agenda for practice is reviewed with visual schedule
Team activity: dribbling (5–10 minutes)	• Coach points to symbols on the visual schedule and says, "Team activity, dribbling." How the kids will practice dribbling is clearly but simply described and demonstrated, "Tap the ball with the inside of your feet," Children practice with volunteers and coaches who provide encouragement and additional demonstration when needed • Coach uses a portable white board to show the players where to move the ball while dribbling • To prevent discouragement, the children are reminded that it is ok to lose control of the ball, "Just go and get it"

cont.

Table 12.1 A typical I CAN Play Soccer lesson *cont.*

Program components	Description
Free time with the soccer ball (5 minutes)	• Referring again to the visual schedule, the coach announces "Team activity, dribbling is over. Now, free time with the soccer ball." Children play independently with the soccer ball or to just take a break and chill out
Team activity: kicking (5–10 minutes)	• Coach announces (and encourages players to repeat), "Break time is over!" • The team activity is introduced, "Team activity: kicking." Kicking is distinguished from dribbling with a brief description and demonstration, "When I kick, I use the top of my foot" The white board is used to show children today's drill
Free time with the soccer ball (5 minutes)	• Another break, as before, children are invited to play with the soccer ball or to just take a break • The coach suggests players get a drink and reminds them that if they need to leave the gym to go to the washroom they need to ask an adult
Team activity: sharing (10 minutes)	• Next activity, "Team activity: sharing" is introduced. Children are told that they can share about anything at all, they can "show" something or "tell" about something • Two or three children are invited to share each week *Note: over the 13-week session, children become more and more familiar with this activity and arrive at the practices with something to share. This activity quickly becomes a favourite for many of the kids, it gives them a way to learn more about each other and make connections of interest beyond soccer*
Free time with the soccer ball (5 minutes)	• Same instructions, as the last break time
Team activity: 3 – 2 – 1 (5–10 minutes)	• The final team activity, 3 – 2 – 1! Children line up at one end of the gym. One at a time, each child lets the coach know if they want the ball kicked "high" or "low" after which they chase after the ball and try to kick it into the goal. A volunteer guards the goal but usually lets in any ball that comes close to the net. Big cheers are modelled and encouraged for all goals or simply for good attempts!
Team cheer and goodbyes (5 minutes)	• Children are acknowledged for all their hard work and asked to come together in a huddle for a team cheer before home time The kids are encouraged to give each other (and the coach and volunteers) "high fives" to formally close the lesson

AN OUTDOOR SOCCER PROGRAM: BLAZIN' SOCCER DOGS

The Blazin' Soccer Dogs was started in 2007 by a parent who was frustrated that her daughter was not included in a community soccer league. When her daughter was denied entry, Abbe Gates wrote to the local newspaper, not to complain, but to see if there was anyone "out there" who would be interested in starting up a soccer program for kids who need extra support. The response from the public was overwhelming – coaches, donations, and volunteers came out of the woodwork. Most importantly, when the newly named Blazin' Soccer Dogs held their first practice about a month later, over 60 children and their families came out to join the program!

Who participates?

Over the past four years the Blazin' Soccer Dogs have welcomed any child aged 4 to 18 years regardless of skill level. The program draws children with many developmental disabilities and many who have ASD. The children are divided into two groups for practice – the "Soccer Pups" who are the younger and less experienced players (usually aged 4 to 8 years) and the "Soccer Dogs" the older, more experienced players (usually aged 9 and over).

Where and when do they play soccer?

The program is held on Saturday mornings for 10-week sessions – once in the spring and once in the fall. Each Saturday, up to 60 players and 60 volunteers descend on the school field. The army of kids, parents, and volunteers are "organized" by several coaches and couple of dedicated parents who register the players and manage the volunteers.

Volunteers are asked to come half an hour before practice, to warm up with a cup of coffee and learn about the practice schedule for the day and who or what they will be supporting. The program recruits volunteers from a local high school that requires their graduates to complete volunteer hours. There is one main coach for the whole group and several junior coaches for the Pups and the Dogs. When parents and their children arrive, they register and the player is matched with a volunteer (there may be several kids with one volunteer, depends on ability). Siblings are also invited to play (and often do!). Check out Table 12.2 for a description of a typical Soccer Dogs lesson.

What do the children learn?

The children learn basic soccer skills, get lots of practice running, and, when ready, play a "scrimage-like" game of soccer, which is an informal game, usually with fewer players on a smaller pitch. Most kids become school playground soccer proficient by the time they leave the program. They each get instruction at their level but are always part of the group that they are assigned to (i.e. Dogs or Pups).

Table 12.2 A typical Blazin' Soccer Dogs lesson

Program components	Description
Volunteer meeting (10 minutes)	• The coach meets with all the volunteers to give them a run down on how the practice will proceed • Drills are described and volunteers are assigned to stations
Field set up (10 minutes)	• Stations are set up to practice drills – usual stations are: dribbling, passing, and shooting. Volunteers are responsible for instructing the drill at that station
Warm up (10 minutes)	• All the players and helpers are called to the field • Everyone participates in a warm up led by the lead coach • After a "team run" around the field, the players break off into Pup and Dog groups
Stations (45 minutes)	• Skill stations for dribbling, shooting, and passing are set up around the field and are manned by junior coaches • Players are split into three groups and rotate around the stations, spending 15 minutes in each
Break time and Pups finish (10 minutes)	• Pups (the younger players) say goodbye – the Dogs give them high fives and congratulate them on a good practice • Players take a break for drinks and snack • Holidays and birthdays are celebrated with special snacks and cheers
Game time (30–40 minutes)	• Three fields are set up – one for each level of play depending on players' skill and experience
Goodbyes (5 minutes)	• Players are encouraged to give each other a hand shake and acknowledge each other for "good soccer" with eye contact and a cheer • The coach lets each player know how well they played and how happy he was to see them come out to practice

Why do we need alternative delivery methods like Soccer Dogs?

This program provides one-to-one support for players when appropriate and does a good job of breaking down the basic soccer skills to help each player become a better player. The lead coach carefully guides the junior coaches and volunteers to provide consistent instruction at the child's level. All the coaches use visual supports, simplified language, and loads of encouragement to move the kids along in their play. To quote one of the coaches, "The skills get better, no matter who they are, every kid can play soccer." There is a dedicated focus on what the participants are doing right, not where they need to improve. The most impressive aspect of this program is the great sense of community it creates for the families. In short, families get more than just soccer from this program. What they get is a real sense of belonging that extends from the coaches, volunteers, players to each member of their family that comes out to play – everyone seems to benefit.

A MOTHER'S STORY: JESSE AND ZACK
Karren Thibeault

Photo 12.2 Zack (left) and Jesse (right)

I have twin boys, Jesse and Zack, who participate in the soccer "I CAN Sports Series" in Vancouver, British Columbia, Canada. My boys are now 16 years old. We started with CAN about two years ago and I can't say enough about what the program has done for my boys.

When Jesse and Zack first started in the program they had very few soccer skills. When they were younger and the other kids were going to soccer and baseball practices, we were very busy with interventions for speech and language, behaviour, and social skills. This left very little time for recreational activities like soccer. As the twins got older we tried to get them involved in team sports, but this didn't work well. The other kids had much more experience and were more advanced than our boys, who were just beginners. Not only did the boys worry about being able to fit in with the group because of their ASD, but they were not able to keep up. This didn't help their self-esteem and made playing sports not much fun.

When CAN started their soccer program it was an answer to our problem! CAN accept children from 5–16 at any skill level. The program gave Jesse and Zack a place where they could learn basic soccer skills and socialize with their peers without the fear of non-acceptance or the worry of competition. The support provided by the coaches and volunteers was invaluable. As the boy's skill level increased, they developed confidence during the practices. This sense of accomplishment was reinforced with the report cards they received after each session. More importantly, Jesse and Zack have made a few friends along the way, guys and gals that they look forward to getting together with at practice each week.

The program has also been a great resource for me, I have connected with the other parents and we have shared stories and also have learned about other activities in the community.

When the boys turned 16 years old last January, they become too old for the soccer program. It had become such a part of our weekly routine that I was distraught about losing our connection to the great coaches and the other kids. I had enjoyed seeing my boys truly enjoying themselves, shining during practice. But, again CAN came through for us: they invited the boys back as peer mentors! This was another opportunity for them to grow and develop – they could help new players learn what they had learned. This has been truly awesome for them! The boys were so proud of themselves and I saw their confidence shoot right up! They have expressed the great pride they take in being program volunteers:

Jesse: Now that I'm a volunteer I can help out kids the same way the program had helped me! Being a peer mentor makes me feel important; we have lots of fun and I really enjoy encouraging the kids and being a role model.

Zack: I am now working as a peer volunteer and I feel great helping the kids out with soccer. I really think that I may be making a difference. It's an amazing feeling having someone look up to you, like how these kids do.

CAN has taken the time to make a place for my boys in their organization and this has meant the world to me. Participation in this soccer program has really made my boys and I feel part of a larger community.

GETTING PREPARED TO PLAY SOCCER FOR THE FIRST TIME

Selecting a soccer program

Finding the right soccer program for your child might take a little leg work. Start by contacting your local community centre and speaking to the person in charge of making their programs accessible. These professionals are usually in tune with which programs in your community provide accommodations and supports for new soccer players with ASD or other developmental disabilities. You may have a choice of joining a soccer program that is designed for players with ASD or other special needs (like the ones we describe in this chapter) or joining a community program that can accommodate the student's needs. You will need to be specific in outlining your child's characteristics to the program director or new coach. In Chapter 3 we provide some suggestions for finding a good coach and ways to help them understand your child. Remember to enquire if the coach has experience with players with ASD and whether there will be any additional staff or volunteers available to help support your child's learning.

The gear: Clothing and equipment

For soccer players who will be playing outside, the following clothing/equipment is recommended.

Shin guards and socks

For team play, shin guards are recommended and in some leagues they are mandatory. Wearing shin guards will prevent bruising from the ball and misdirected kicks. Wearing shin guards from the start so that they become a part of the everyday soccer wardrobe works best for most players with ASD. In order to keep them in place, it is best to wear long socks. Socks that fit well are very important. Some people don't like to wear socks at all. But, wearing them during soccer play is encouraged to prevent blisters from developing on the player's feet.

Soccer shoes/cleats

Soccer shoes are sturdy, light shoes with rubber or plastic bumps (called "cleats") on the sole of the shoe. Cleats help the child gain traction on the field, making running easier and slipping less likely. Soccer shoes usually lace up so help may be needed to get them on and tie the laces. Some leagues have a stockpile of "old" cleats that they collect from season to season which you may be able to access.

Team uniform

While it is great to have a uniform to help create a team identity, this isn't always necessary. Some leagues will have players come in their own clothes and then make use of two sets of "pinnies" in contrasting colours to identify teams. Photos 12.4 (a) and (b) show a child in a pinny and a child in a complete uniform consisting of co-ordinated socks, shorts, and soccer jersey.

Photo 12.3 Soccer cleats from Soccer Dogs

INDOOR SOCCER

All that's needed for indoor soccer are comfortable runners and clothes that are light and loose so running is possible without getting overheated. Beginner indoor soccer players do not wear traditional soccer cleats and typically do not need shin guards. The "play" in indoor soccer is usually a lot slower and less potentially dangerous, because of the use of a low-bounce ball. There are a couple of low-bounce balls. The old style low-bounce balls are like giant tennis balls – they have soft felt on the outside and are not as inflated as regular soccer balls. What is more commonly used today is a "Futsal" ball – these balls are smaller than a typical soccer ball and have low bounce because the bladder is filled with foam. Indoor soccer balls are easier to handle and ideal for beginner indoor practices where the ball is not kicked as far. They are also great for kids who kick with a bit too much power (a regular bounce ball might put others in danger) and for those who need a slower ball to perfect emerging ball handling skills.

(a)   (b)

Photo 12.4 Soccer clothing

Play around with a ball in your backyard or neighbourhood park

Messing around with a soccer ball in the back yard is a great thing to do before you head off for your first soccer practice. Most kids with ASD have spent time playing turn-taking games with interventionists, teachers, parents, and siblings. Passing a soccer ball back and forth is another way to extend these familiar activities. To start, use this time to model gently kicking the ball with your feet and encouraging your child to do the same. Make sure you get into the groove of your child's interest with the ball, copying his actions while you encourage him or her to copy yours. Gradually extend the time playing. Also remember to use "soccer talk" (see Table 12.3) to begin to familiarize him or her with the instructional language that he or she will soon be exposed to at practice (e.g. "Thanks for *passing* me the *soccer* ball! What a great *kick*!").

Learn the lingo: Soccer talk

There are lots of new words to learn to play soccer! When you are just starting out, it is pretty simple. Kids need to know how to take direction from the coach and learn to handle the ball. They can wait until they are more advanced to learn all the positions, the details about the field, and the rules of the game. Below are some basic terms to get started with.

Table 12.3 Soccer talk: Vocabulary for on the field

Soccer terms	Skills	Body parts/ gear	Equipment	Instructional language
Drill	Dribble	Foot/feet	Ball	"Everyone on the line!"
Game	Kicking	Legs	Cone	
Scoring	Passing	Shin guards and socks	Disc	"Look up"
Team	Shooting		Goal	"Side of your foot"
Warm up	Trapping the ball	Soccer shoes	Net	
		Uniform or pinnie		"Top of your foot"
				"Watch the ball"

Take a tour of the field or gym practice location

For some kids with ASD, having a visit to the facility or field where the practices will be held is a good idea. For other children, this isn't as necessary but may serve as another language learning opportunity. Make sure you gauge your player's level of comfort with the practice location. If your athlete takes time to get used to new environments, you might want to take a few pictures of the new setting and spend some time each day talking about the upcoming soccer practice. Below is an example of a simple "soccer book" that could be used to help a child become more relaxed and comfortable with this new experience. Like a social story, the pictures simply prepare the new player to become familiar with the people, place, and activities expected with this new activity.

YOUR FIRST EXPERIENCE: CHECKLIST

Luckily, there's not much gear that you need to jump into your first soccer practice! However, we have covered a number of strategies to help you prepare your student for fun on the field. Do you have everything you need? Let's check.

My soccer checklist

To do	Done!
Spoken to coach and/or program co-ordinator	❏
Have the gear for outdoor soccer or loose and comfortable clothing for indoor soccer. Make sure you take a water bottle!	❏
Practiced with the soccer ball	❏
Reviewed soccer talk	❏
Visited the practice location	❏
You're ready to play soccer!	

Figure 12.1 Soccer priming story

COACHES' CORNER: YOU NEED A GAME PLAN

Coaches need to have a very good "game plan" before they start up a "learn to play" soccer program. From the first practice onward, they need to establish clear routines, supported by simple and clear language with lots of visual supports. Figure 12.1 is an example of an individualized "primary" story that can help a child to understand what will occur at soccer practice. Warnings for transitions need to be clearly made. To instruct the players in a group, we found that coaches call players to a "team meeting," which is a cue that there will be important information to listen to. Cone and discs to mark out drills are used in most skill instruction. Additionally, using a white board to sketch out how the players will move through a drill is helpful. Coaches need to work in lots of breaks and let the kids keep up at their own pace. Above all "keep it simple!" and keep it positive!

One more thing, be patient. Many new players will be reluctant to be "on the move" for an entire hour of practice, so it is important to figure out the comfort level of the group and, if possible, each player. There should be no expectation that all players will "practice" for the full hour of the class, and remember, shorter activities lead to better attention spans.

:ʘ: **TIP** Instructional language – avoid saying "Can you…?" because this gives the option of "No!" A better strategy is to give a choice. For example, "Would you like to kick the ball with the disc or without the disc?"

Photo 12.5 White board

PREPARING FOR YOUR FIRST TIME ON THE FIELD

Equipment

There are a number of different pieces of equipment used in a soccer game. Let's check them out.

Soccer ball

There are several sizes of soccer balls and a couple of types. An official soccer ball is 27 to 28 inches round (68 to 71cm) and weighs 14 to 16 ounces (390 to 450g). In many kids programs, *smaller soccer balls* are used (10 to 12 ounces, or 280 to 340g). These balls are both lighter and smaller making them easier for smaller feet to control. Professional soccer balls are hand-sewn and made of soft leather, they last longer than cheaper rubber or nylon balls. However, expense is an important consideration when you need to have many balls available for practices. A good option for indoor games are *low-bounce balls*, these have soft felt on the outside and are not as inflated as other balls. These balls are easier to handle and ideal for:

- beginner indoor practices where the ball is not kicked as far

- for players who kick harder (a regular bounce ball might put others in danger)

- for those whose ball handling skills are just beginning to develop.

Net

On a regulation 100- to 130-yard field (92 to 120m), the net or goal is 8 yards (7.3m) wide and 8 feet (244cm) high. There are two nets, one at each end of the field. The net is stretched between two goalposts and an upper crossbar. For children who are just learning to play soccer, smaller collapsible nets are often used to demarcate a smaller field or to set up other "net" configurations for practice drills.

Cones and discs

For practices, orange traffic cones and flat discs are used to facilitate a variety of drills. The discs are handy to use to place and steady balls for kicking practice (see Photo 12.6), and the cones can be set up in many configurations for various dribbling and passing drills.

Photo 12.6 Cones and discs

WARM UP AND BASIC SOCCER SKILLS

Soccer is a sport that is fast and active. Players need to get in shape in order to enjoy playing because the game involves running, kicking, passing, more running, and scoring goals. So, general fitness is important, but in order to prepare the body to get ready for action, you need to warm up your muscles. This helps prevent injuries and gets some oxygen flowing to the brain so that the mind is ready to make good decisions about the ball and other players.

Warm up

A warm up is usually part of every soccer practice. It gives you a chance to practice your soccer actions and get your muscles and brain ready to do lots of running and learning ball skills. Warm up routines can be very simple, involving imitation exercises led by the coach or more complicated group activities. For the new player with ASD, it is important that they know "warm up" is an essential part of each practice.

SIMPLE DYNAMIC WARM UP ACTIVITIES

Follow the leader
The coach begins to run in a small circle, he or she calls one child's name at a time to follow him or her, children run in a line until the last child is called. All moves are conducted while following the leader.

1. Knees to hands – children raise knees to hands warming up the quadriceps.
2. Heels to bum – change the move, warming up the hamstrings!
3. Walk on toes – works on balance.
4. Swing your arms – warms up the shoulders.
5. Swing straight legs – works on hip flexion and leg control.
6. Big arm circles – more shoulders.

One more run fast, then slow.

Photo 12.7 Warm up

Basic ball handling skills

The most basic skill to learn in soccer is how to handle the ball. There are several ball handling skills. Check out Table 12.4 for a quick reference list of the basic skills. The most basic are dribbling and kicking (which also includes passing to another player and shooting to a target). With all ball handling skills the player needs to learn three things: (1) how to make *good contact*, (2) how to become *more accurate*, and (3) how to get *good power*. Players are encouraged to practice each skill with both feet to become more "balanced" players. If players can't use both feet they overcompensate with the more dominant foot getting into all kinds of awkward positions just to kick the ball with the "good" foot. Mastering basic skills with both feet will set most players up to play a good game of scrimmage. We will review the basic skills of dribbling, kicking, passing, and shooting in this section.

Table 12.4 Basic ball handling skills at a glance

Type of movement or skill	Basic skill	Next steps
Dribbling	Passing ball back and forth on the insides of the feet while standing in one spot – "tippy tappy"	Pass ball back and forth between feet while moving forward up the field
Kicking	While a volunteer holds the ball on the ground, the player practices the motion of kicking. After practicing with one foot, turn around and practice with the other foot	The ball is placed on a disc (a still or "dead" ball) and the player kicks the ball. Next, one foot away from the ball, step forward and kick
Passing (kicking to a person)	While standing still, kick the ball to a partner who is standing close	Kick the ball to a partner that is standing further away
Shooting (kicking to a target)	Kick the "still" ball at a close wall target	Back up to make the target smaller, and kick

SIMPLE SOCCER INSTRUCTIONAL CUES

Sometimes it's difficult to describe the physical movements that are a part of soccer. Let's take a look at some of the instruction language or cues that could be used when introducing these basic ball skills.

Basic ball skills

Skills	Instructional cue
Dribbling	"Tap the ball with the inside of your foot to your other foot. And back again"
Passing	"Look at the person you will pass to. Kick the ball with the inside part of the foot"
Shooting	"Look at where you will shoot the ball. Kick the ball with inside part of your foot" Fancy stuff: " To get a hard shot – kick with the top part of your foot"

Dribbling

Soccer players move the ball on the field by dribbling. This is a tricky skill to learn as children have to co-ordinate jogging forward while tapping the ball with their foot to keep control of it. Learning to do this well can take years. Some players might start by using only one foot to tap the ball forward but it is best to encourage them to use both feet from the start. Eventually, they have to tap the ball with the inside of their foot with their left and right foot, change directions in mid stride and change speeds to avoid opposing players when they get into team play.

So how do you get started when you're first learning to dribble? Start off standing still. Have the new player stand with their feet hip-distance apart with the ball leaning up against one foot. Have the player practice gently passing the ball back and forth between their feet, right to left and left to right.

TIP Remember balance – it is easier to learn to dribble if children are close to the ground – encourage bent knees and loose arms!

Next, from your hip-width stance, try pushing the ball slightly forward and across the body (e.g. from the right foot, forward in front of the left foot). Then, using this example, step the left foot forward to meet the ball. Continue moving slowly forward first pushing the ball with small kick across the body and then stepping forward to meet the ball with the other foot.

💡**TIP** Encourage players to use short quick steps when dribbling. As your student becomes more comfortable with this left to right motion and the idea of moving forward up the field, you can begin to increase the force of the push and begin to quicken the pace of the movement between the pushes between feet. Now you're dribbling!

(a)   (b)

Photo 12.8 Dribbling

Kicking

New players are taught to kick the ball with the instep of their foot, or the inside of the foot The instep – or where your laces are – allows for better control than your toes and also is less likely to cause injury to the foot. Let's look at a simple three-step method to practice kicking:

1. Place your standing foot beside the ball and stand in the direction you want to hit the ball.

2. Using your kicking foot, strike the back of the ball with your shoelaces.

3. After kicking, let your striking foot follow-through in the direction you want to hit the ball.

Kicking drill

All you need is a ball and a wall. If you strike the ball correctly, it should come right back to you. Start close to the wall, do the basic kick, move back as you get better. Remember to practice with both feet!

Photo 12.9 Kicking

Passing

Moving the ball to other players is an important part of the game. Learning to pass well – with just enough power and directional control – is what moves soccer from an individual sport to a team sport. When beginning to pass, players are typically taught to use the instep of the foot, to hit the ball, and follow-through with the foot in the direction that the ball needs to go.

TIP Kicking hard and soft. Sometimes passing is difficult for some players because they kick the ball too hard. To learn what "soft" kicking means, get the players to kick the ball into a hula hoop – they have to kick it SOFT to just make it into the circle and not over the other side.

TIP To learn to pass accurately children can pass to another player by kicking the ball between two cones. As their passing improves, move the cones closer together.

TRAPPING

Although this may seem counterintuitive, learning to "trap" the ball, or stop it as it comes toward you is a fairly advanced skill for most new players. But being able to stop the ball when it comes close increases ball control during passing or shooting, so some players who have good co-ordination can be taught this skill. One of the simplest ways to control the ball is to "trap it" with the sole of your foot. However, this requires co-ordination as well as balance and can take a bit of practice to get the hang of. Trapping can be practiced with a partner by:

- standing face to face with a partner about 5 feet (150cm) apart
- have the player slightly raise his or her foot off the ground or tilt the toe upward leaving the heel of the foot on the ground (easier for bigger feet)
- as the partner, gently kick or roll the ball to the new player as he or she watches the ball slowly approach
- have the player firmly push his or her foot on top of the ball to "trap" it.

TIP Stopping the ball. Another way to stop the ball is to keep your eye on it as it approaches you and stop it with the inside of your still foot. The large inside surface of your foot acts to cushion the ball to make it easier to control.

> **TIP** WAITING to pass. Passing is hard for some kids because it involves waiting for the partner to be ready to receive the ball. Players are invited to call out, "READY?" and to hear back from their partner, "READY!" before they pass the ball.

Shooting

Shooting, like passing, involves accuracy but typically the target is not another team mate but the goal! Shooting also calls for a kick with a lot of power, so new players are taught to run up to the ball, place their non-kicking foot beside the ball, and, with the kicking foot, strike the ball with the laces of the shoe. Players are taught to keep the ankle rigid and to follow-through by swinging the leg forward. Landing with balance on the kicking foot is an important next step for children to learn. As with ball handling skills, beginners should learn to shoot with either foot, but this takes practice as most kids start off with a preference for the foot that they kick with or a "dominant foot."

Photo 12.10 Shooting

> 💡**TIP** The POWER shot. Most players require a lot of practice to get their foot underneath the ball to lift it up into the air, initially this can be achieved by using the plastic discs to place the ball on to keep it stable and somewhat raised in the air. With repeated practice, and concentrating on hitting the ball with the correct part of the foot (the laces) and then following through, children improve their shooting precision.

GAME TIME

Learning all the parts of the field is usually not the most important aspect of learning to play soccer for most new players, the basic moves that help you handle the ball with control, accuracy, and power are usually where coaches begin. After new players begin to master ball skills, it is usually time to introduce a "mini" soccer game or "scrimage." When players learn how to actually "play" a soccer game for the first time, it is best to keep the team small, the field small, and the rules super simple. This way, all players will be more involved, not get too frustrated or tired, and will experience more ball contact.

Players

For very small kids, three versus three on a small field is a good number to start with. For slightly older or more able kids, teams of six that play two halves for only 25 minutes works well. Limiting the types of positions is a good idea too. A goalkeeper, a couple of defensive players, and two or three forwards are enough to keep the game rolling!

Field of play

For these beginners, a good field size might be 50 yards (46m) long and 30 yards (28m) wide. A simple picture of the field, with a few key features noted (e.g. the goals, the centre line, the centre spot, out of bounds, and corner kick spots) makes a great handout to give to a child with ASD the week before his first game (see Figure 12.2). Orientation to the field and the positions helps introduce players to the upcoming new experience of playing a game.

Rules

It is also important to keep the rules simple. Here is an example of "simple" rules that work well for mini soccer games:

- MOST IMPORTANTLY, points are scored by putting the ball in the other team's goal.

- Only the goalie can touch the ball with his or her hands.

- When the ball goes outside the field, it should be kicked in by a player of the opposite team.

WHEN CAN WE TRY MORE ADVANCED SOCCER SKILLS?

It is clear to most experienced coaches when it is time to introduce more advanced skills. These skills might include improved co-ordination with the ball, trickier passes, more complex teamwork practice, tackling to get the ball away from an opponent, and playing the various positions within a game. Once you have found a good program with a coach who understands how to support your child take the coach's advice on when and how your new player should progress in the sport.

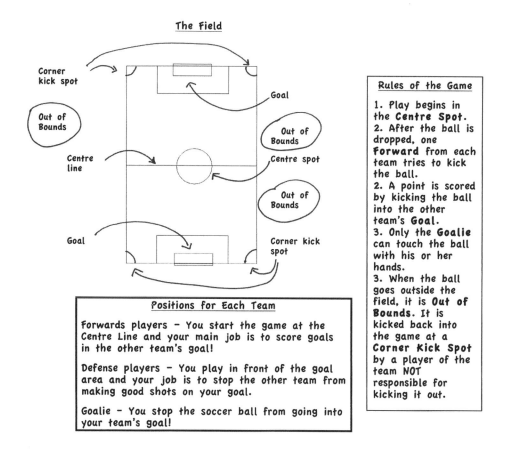

Figure 12.2 Mini soccer game: Field, positions (and definitions), and rules of the game

SUMMING UP

In this chapter, we've really only covered the basics when it comes to learning how to play soccer. We've described two examples of programs that provide excellent introductions of soccer to players with ASD. We hope that you can use these programs as models for setting up your own programs and introduce new young players with ASD to this wonderful sport.

Photo 12.11 End of game hand circle

RESOURCES

Examples of learn to play soccer programs

Australia

Grasshopper Soccer
    www.grasshoppersoccer.com.au

Canada

Canadian Soccer Association
    www.canadasoccer.com

I CAN Play Soccer (British Columbia)
    http://canucksautism.ca

Blazin' Soccer Dogs (Vancouver, BC)
    http://soccerdogs.ca

New Zealand

New Zealand Football
www.nzfootball.co.nz/index.php?id=3

United Kingdom

Arsenal Soccer Schools
www.playthearsenalway.com

Manchester United Soccer Schools
www.englishandsoccer.co.uk

United States

US Soccer Federation
www.ussoccer.com

Shooting Stars Soccer Program (New Jersey)
www.soccerlearningcenter.com

Note: for more information on the Canucks Autism Network sport programs go to http://canucksautism.ca.

ACKNOWLEDGMENT

In writing this chapter, Veronica benefited from the editorial assistance of many gifted soccer coaches. She would like to acknowledge the contributions and editorial guidance of Greg Poirier, Ryan Yao, and Nish Lal.

REFERENCES

American Red Cross (2004) *Swimming and Water Safety.* Yardley, PA: StayWell.

Bachrach, A.W., Mosley, A.R., Swindle, F.L. and Wood, M.W. (1978) *Developmental Therapy for Young Children with Autistic Characteristics.* Baltimore, MD: University Park Press.

Baranek, G.T. (2002) "Efficacy of sensory and motor intervention for children with autism." *Journal of Autism and Developmental Disabilities 32,* 397–422.

Bauminger, N. and Kasari, C. (2000) "Loneliness and friendship in high-functioning children with autism." *Child Development 71,* 447–456.

Best, J.F. and Jones, J.G. (1972) "Movement therapy in the treatment of autistic children." *Australian Occupational Therapy Journal 21,* 72–86.

Bondy, A.S. and Frost, L.A. (1994) "The picture exchange communication system." *Focus on Autism and Other Developmental Disabilities 9,* 1–19.

British Taekwondo Control Board (2011) *What is Taekwondo?* Available at www.britishtaekwondo.org.uk/what-is-taekwondo.html.

Burtton, D. and Martens, R. (1986) "Pinned by their own goals: An exploratory investigation into why kids drop out of wrestling." *Journal of Sport Psychology 8,* 183–197.

Canadian Sport for Life (2011) *Canadian Sport for Life: Long Term Athlete Development, Resource Paper, v2.* Available at www.canadiansportforlife.ca/resources/ltad-resource-papers.

Centers for Disease Control and Prevention (2012) "Autism Spectrum Disorders (ASDs): Data and Statistics." Available at www.cdc.gov/ncbddd/autism/data.html.

Curtin, C., Anderson, S.E., Must, A. and Bandini, L. (2010) "The prevalence of obesity in children with autism: A secondary data analysis using nationally representative data from the National Survey of Children's Health." *BioMed Central Pediatrics 10,* 1471–2431.

Dalrymple, N.J. (1995) "Environmental Supports to Develop Flexibility and Independence." In K.A. Quill (ed.) *Teaching Children with Autism: Strategies to Enhance Communication and Socialization.* New York: Delmar Publishers Inc.

Dettmer, S., Simpson, R.L., Smith Myles, B. and Ganz, J.B. (2000) "The use of visual supports to facilitate transitions of students with autism." *Focus on Autism and Other Developmental Disabilities 15,* 163–169.

Finkenberg, M. (1990) "Effect of participation in Taekwondo on college women's self concept." *Perceptual and Motor Skills 71*, 891–894.

Fuller, J. (1988) "Martial arts and physiological health." *British Journal of Medical Psychology 61*, 317–328.

Gillmeister, H. (1997) *Tennis: A Cultural History.* London: Leicester University Press.

Grandin, T. (1995) *Thinking in Pictures: And Other Reports from My Life with Autism.* New York: Random House, Inc.

Hamilton, A. (1972) "Learning to talk while developing motor skills." *Journal of Health, Physical Education and Recreation 43*, 80–81.

Haskell, W.L., Lee, I.M., Pate, R.R., Powell, K.E. *et al.* (2007) "Physical activity and public health: Updated recommendations for adults from the American college of sports medicine and the American heart association." *Medicine and Science in Sports and Exercise 39*, 1423–1434.

Hilton, C.L. (2011) "Sensory Processing and Motor Disorders in Autism Spectrum Disorders." In J.L. Matson and P. Sturmey (eds) *International Handbook of Autism and Pervasive Developmental Disorders.* New York: Springer Publishers.

Janzen, J.E. (2009) *Autism Handbook for Parents: Facts and Strategies for Parenting Success.* Waco, TX: Prufrock Press Inc.

Jasmin, E., Couture, M., McKinley, P., Reid, G., Fombonne, E. and Gisel, E. (2009) "Sensori-motor and daily living skills of preschool children with autism spectrum disorders." *Journal of Autism and Developmental Disorders 39*, 231–241.

Kasari, C., Rotheram-Fuller, E., Locke, J. and Gulsrud, A. (2012) "Making the Connection: Randomized controlled trial of social skills at school for children with autism spectrum disorders." *Journal of Child Psychology and Psychiatry 53*, 431–439.

Kohl, H.W. and Hobbs, K.E. (1998) "Development of physical activity behaviors among children and adolescents." *Pediatrics 101*, 549–554.

Kurian, M., Caterino, L. and Kulhavy, R. (1993) "Personality characteristics and duration of ATA Taekwondo training." *Perceptual and Motor Skills 76*, 363–366.

Kurtz, L.A. (2007) *Understanding Motor Skills in Children with Dyspraxia, ADHD, Autism, and Other Learning Disabilities: A Guide to Improving Coordination.* London: Jessica Kingsley Publishers.

Law, M., King, G., King, S., Kertoy, M., *et al.* (2007) *Patterns and Predictors of Recreational and Leisure Participation for Children with Physical Disabilities.* Published online by CanChild Centre for Childhood Disability Research. McMaster University, Hamilton, ON. Available at www.canchild.ca/en/canchildresources/patternsandpredictors.asp.

Lee, I.M. and Paffenbarger, R.S. (2000) "Associations of light, moderation, and vigorous intensity physical activity with longevity." *American Journal of Epidemiology 151*, 293–299.

Lee, T.D. and Schmidt, R.P. (1999) *Motor Control and Learning: A Behavioural Emphasis.* Champaign, IL: Human Kinetics.

Lewis, M. and Lalas, A. (2000) *Soccer for Dummies.* Indianapolis, IN: Wiley Publishing.

Marr, D., Mika, H., Miraglia, J., Roerig, M. and Sinnott, R. (2007) "The effect of sensory stories on targeted behaviors in preschool children with autism." *Physical and Occupational Therapy in Pediatrics 27*, 63–79.

Matson, J.L. and Boisjoli, J.A. (2009) "The token economy for children with intellectual disability and/or autism: A review." *Research in Developmental Disabilities 30*, 240–248.

McDuffie, A. and Yoder, P. (2010) "Types of parent verbal responsiveness that predict language in young children with autism spectrum disorder." *Journal of Speech, Language, and Hearing Research 53*, 1026–1039.

Ministry of Industry (2009) *Caring Canadians, Involved Canadians: Highlights from the 2007 Canada Survey of Giving, Volunteering and Participating*. Available at www.givingandvolunteering.ca/files/giving/en/csgvp_highlights_2007.pdf.

Pan, C.-Y. (2008) "Objectively measured physical activity between children with autism spectrum disorders and children without disabilities during inclusive recess settings in Taiwan." *Journal of Autism and Developmental Disorders 38*, 1292–1301.

Pan, C.-Y. (2011) "The efficacy of an aquatic program on physical fitness and aquatic skills in children with autism spectrum disorders." *Research in Autism Spectrum Disorders 5*, 657–665.

Pan, C.-Y. and Frey, C. (2006) "Physical activity patterns in youth with autism spectrum disorders." *Journal of Autism and Developmental Disabilities 36*, 597–606.

Rogers, L., Hemmeter, M.L. and Wolery, M. (2010) "Using a constant time delay procedure to teach foundational swimming skills to children with autism." *Topics in Early Childhood Special Education 30*, 102–111.

Rosser, D.D. and Frey, C. (2005) "Comparison of physical activity levels between children with and without autism spectrum disorders." *Adapted Physical Activity Quarterly 22*, 146–159.

Schleien, S., Ray, M. and Green, F. (1997) *Community Recreation and People with Disabilities: Strategies for Inclusion* (2nd edn). Baltimore, WA: Brookes.

Sibley, B.A. and Etnier, J.L. (2003) "The relationship between physical activity and cognition in children: A meta-analysis." *Pediatric Exercise Science 15*, 243–256.

Skard, O. and Vaglum, P. (1989) "The influence of psychosocial and sport factors on dropout from boys' soccer: A prospective study." *Scandinavian Journal of Sports Science 11*, 65–72.

Stone, W.L., Ousley, O.Y., Hepburn, S.L., Hogan, K.L. and Brown, C.S. (1999) "Patterns of adaptive behavior in very young children with autism." *American Journal on Mental Retardation 104*, 187–199.

Tissot, C. and Evans, R. (2003) "Visual teaching strategies for children with autism." *Early Child Development and Care 173*, 425–433.

Tomporowski, P.D. (1986) "Effects of exercise on cognitive processes: A review." *Psychology Bulletin 99*, 338–346.

Torbert, M. (2011) *Secrets to Success in Sport and Play: A Practical Guide to Skill Development*. Chicago, IL: Human Kinetics.

Trost S.G., Pate, R.R., Sallis, J.F., Freedson, P.S., *et al.* (2002) "Age and gender differences in objectively measured physical activity in youth." *Medicine and Science in Sports and Exercises 34*, 350–355.

Twemlow, S.W., Biggs, B.K., Nelson, T.D., Vernberg, E.M., Fonagy, P. and Twemlow, S.W. (2008) "Participation in a martial arts-based antibullying program in elementary schools." *Psychology in the Schools 45*, 1–13.

US Department of Health (2008) *Physical Activity Guidelines for Americans.* Washington, DC: Government Printing Office, October 2008. Available at www.health.gov/paguidelines/pdf/paguide.pdf.

US Department of Health and Human Services (2002) *Healthy People 2010*, 2nd edn, with "Understanding and improving health" and "Objectives for improving health," two vols. Washington, DC: Government Printing Office, November 2000.

US Soccer Federation (2000) "History of Soccer." Available at www.ussoccer.com.

Weiss, M.R. and Ferrer-Caja, E. (2002) "Motivational Orientations and Sport Behavior." In T. Horn (ed.) *Advances in Sport Psychology* (2nd edn). Champaign, IL: Human Kinetics.

Wetherby, A.M. (2006) "Understanding and Measuring Social Communication in Children with Autism Spectrum Disorders." In T. Charman and W. Stone (eds) *Social and Communication Development in Autism Spectrum Disorders: Early Identification, Diagnosis and Intervention.* New York: Guilford Press.

Yilmaz, I., Birkan, B., Konukman, F. and Erkan, M. (2004) "Using Constant Time Delay Procedure to Teach Aquatic Play Skills for Children with Autism." *Education and Training in Autism and Developmental Disabilities 40*, 2, 171–182.

Yilmaz, I., Konukman, F., Birkan, B. and Yanardag, M. (2010) "The Effects of Most to Least Prompting on Teaching Simple Progression Swimming Skill for Children with Autism." *Education and Training in Autism and Developmental Disabilities 45*, 3, 440–448.

ABOUT THE AUTHORS

VERONICA SMITH, PHD

Veronica grew up in semi-rural Canada in the 1960s where she spent many hours in a variety of organized and not so organized sports. She learned to skate on a frozen pond, where she acted as goalie for her brother's vicious slap shots, and learned to swim and play soccer in community programs. Through these pursuits she explored her neighbourhood independently, became skilled at learning how to play with others, and developed friendships that followed her to school and into adulthood. She did not stand by and watch others, she participated in and felt part of her community, and, along the way, developed skills and abilities that amused her through childhood and continue to give her unabated pleasure in adulthood. Veronica is now a university professor of special education at the University of Alberta in Edmonton, Canada.

STEPHANIE PATTERSON, MED

Stephanie grew up in Canada spending many hours in the skating rink as an athlete and later as a certified figure skating coach. Through Stephanie's experience in figure skating and additionally in recreational school sports leagues, she discovered the value of sports and appreciated how skilled coaches contributed to her growth and development. After encountering the need for skating coaches who would include children with an array of special developmental needs, she decided to combine her interests in special education and figure skating by providing group skating lessons designed for new and more advanced skaters with special learning needs. Stephanie is currently a doctoral student in psychological studies in education at the University of California in Los Angeles, CA.

THE CONTRIBUTORS

LAURA DUMAS

Laura has a passion for working and teaching children of all ages in a variety of different environments. Having taught swimming lessons since 1998, she developed and taught the SwimAbilities program since 2008 to help address a need for specialized swimming lessons for children with special needs within her local community, Edmonton, Alberta in Canada. Laura earned her Bachelor of Education and taught for three years before going on to obtain her Master of Science degree in Occupational Therapy. As an occupational therapist, Laura's main focus since 2010 has been working specifically with children with ASD, where she further adapted the SwimAbilities program to meet the needs of a greater range of children with special needs. Laura continues to work toward expanding the SwimAbilities program to other communities.

JANINE HADAYKO

Janine is a physiotherapist who enjoys working with children and with adults with developmental disabilities. In 2001, Janine first created the concept of a biking group to help children feel more supported as they seek to master this skill. With the help of John Collier, the Edmonton Bicycle Commuters Society, and a number of dedicated volunteers, this group has improved and expanded into "You Can Ride Two": a free, inclusive program that has helped over a hundred children between the ages of 7 and 14 learn how to ride a two-wheeled bicycle. At the request of some of her colleagues in other communities, she also developed a "train the trainer" course; the graduates of this course are now helping children across Alberta take their first ride without training wheels. Janine's next endeavours are helping to co-ordinate an adapted bicycle loan pool, modifying the program to serve adults with special needs, and pursuing a Master of Science degree with a focus on cycling.

STEPHANIE JULL

Stephanie Jull is a PhD Candidate at the University of British Columbia and a Board Certified Behaviour Analyst (BCBA). For her dissertation research project, she taught local swimming instructors in community pools strategies for teaching children with ASD. The project was very successful and Stephanie continues to provide support and training to several recreation centres throughout Greater Vancouver. She also provides consulting support to recreation programs through Canucks Autism Network and teaches several courses in the ABA-Autism program at Capilano University. Stephanie contributed to parts of Chapter 4, "Learning Supports for Children with Autism."

VIVIAN NG

Vivian first became interested in ASD while working as an aide for children with ASD as she completed her Bachelor of Science degree in Occupational Therapy at the University of Alberta. She began her career at a community agency providing services to children with ASD while continuing her studies, obtaining her Master of Science degree in Occupational Therapy. In her thesis she examined the roles of occupational therapists working with children in community settings. Vivian has worked as a clinician in an Early Education Program within the school setting, and is currently working in the healthcare system with children and adolescents with both complex medical and mental health concerns. Sports have always been a part of Vivian's life and she has experience in many, ranging from skating and skiing, to karate, swimming, and soccer. Introduced to skating at a young age, Vivian developed a passion for the sport and was excited to combine her interests in skating and occupational therapy in co-facilitating a successful and meaningful learn to skate program for families of children and teens with ASD. Vivian provided insightful OT and editorial advice in many of the sports focused chapters.

SHAFALI SPURLING JESTE AND RICHARD SPURLING

A child neurologist focused on developmental disorders and a tennis professional with an MBA in entrepreneurship merged their interests and talents to create ACEing Autism. Through her clinical practice, Shafali Jeste witnessed first hand the paucity of affordable services available to children with autism, especially those centred on sports. Richard Spurling, as a tennis professional, had a particular affinity for junior program development and sought to apply those skills by helping children in need. Shortly after Shafali and Richard were married, they recognized that they could combine their skills to create a meaningful organization that provided tennis lessons for children with autism. Since its creation, ACEing Autism has grown to five sites in the greater Boston and Los Angeles areas. The program services over 100 children with autism of all ages and levels of functioning.

JONATHAN RIVERO, BSC.OT, 4TH DAN BLACKBELT

As my disabled dad lay down in his bed and I stood practicing my daily afternoon calisthenics at the tender age of two, we would ritualistically watch Bruce Lee movies. Bruce often said, "Empty your mind, be formless, shapeless – like water. You put water in a cup, it becomes the cup; put water into a bottle it becomes the bottle; put it in a teapot it becomes the teapot. Now water can flow or it can crash. Be water, my friend." As I cherish the 19 years of my life that I shared with my dad, these words of wisdom have not only been a guide but a life lesson in how he was able to survive living with a brain tumour. He had to give up his occupation of being a physician due to his illness and experts said that he would only live one year. However, he never gave up the occupation of sharing the gift that he still had to offer his family: the gift of being a master in adapting to life and being true to himself. Martial arts gave my dad daily magic moments of healing and meaning with his family. This is dedicated to you, Dad: for who I have become, for what I do, and what I have to offer the world.

SUBJECT INDEX

Page numbers in *italics* refer to figures and tables

academic benefits, of sports 21–2
Access Co-ordinators 37
ACEing Autism program 189–91, *192*
activity patterns 23–4
adult support, for swimming 157, 160
anxiety, decreasing 74, 102, 107, 130, 153
arm bands, for swimming 150
arm's length, keeping at 69
ASD (autism spectrum disorder), diagnosis statistics 10
assertion 69, *70*

backward movement, while skating 133
balance 57–61
    activities 59
    establishing a base of support 57–9, *58*
    and weight transfer 59–61
    while biking 114
ball skills
    in soccer 230, *230*
    in tennis 197–8
balls
    soccer 227
    tennis 195
basic skills tables
    for biking *109*
    for skating *133*
    for soccer *230*
    for swimming *155*
    for taekwondo *177*
    for tennis *200*
behaviour scripts 67, *68*
bells, for bikes 103
benefits, of sports
    for kids of any age 19–22
    for kids with ASD 10–11, 25–6
biking 93–119
    advanced skills 117–18
        figure eights 117
        hills 117
        passing other bikes 118
        shoulder checks 117

balance and weight transfer 61
basic skills 108–16, *109*
    balancing 114
    braking 109–11, *110, 111*
    falling 113
    gliding and coasting 114–15, *115*
    pedalling 115–16, 117
    ready position 111–12, *112*
    steering 112–14
benefits 93–5
choosing the right bike 99–102
    fitting a bike 100, *100*
    other adjustments 100
    size 99
    tips 101–2
first time on a bike 104–8
    bike matching game 106
    bike preparation 108
    biking terms 105, *105*
    checklist 108
    getting on and off 108
    helmets 104
    lesson location 107
    pedalling and steering 104–5
    visual support 107, *107*
other apparel and equipment 103–4
    bells 103
    clothing 103
    training wheels 104
personal story 97–8
practicing 116
preparation 99–104
program example 95–8, *96*
protective gear 102–3
    helmets 102, *103*
    padding 102
rules of the road 118
success strategies 99
tandem bikes 111
Blazin' Soccer Dogs program 216–19
body, learning to move the 55–6
bowing, while doing martial arts 183, *183*
box, thinking outside the 40–2
brain, sports as an aid to functioning 21

braking, while biking 109–11, *110*, *111*
breathing, while doing martial arts 174, 178–9, *178*
bubbles, blowing, while swimming 154–6, *155*

CanSkate™ program 121, 123
Canucks Autism Network (CAN) 212–16
caps, for swimming 150
checklists
   for biking 108
   for martial arts 176
   for skating 132
   for soccer 225
   for swimming 154
   for tennis 200
   for volunteers 84
choosing a sport 28–38
   overcoming hesitancy to enrol 28–35
   questions to consider 36–8
cleats, for soccer shoes 221, *222*
clothing
   for biking 103
   for martial arts 174
   for skating 127
   for soccer 221–2, *222*, *223*
   for swimming 148–9
   for tennis 194–5
coaches
   different kinds of 47–51
   finding the right 45–7
   observation cheat sheet *48*
   qualities of 39–45
   soccer
      game plan 226, *226*
      safety issues for 228
   and volunteers 86–8
   working with 39–53
coasting, while biking 114–15, *115*
communication goals 25
communities
   availability of sports programs 37–8
   involvement of kids with ASD 25
   knowledge of ASD within 26
   volunteers and 86–7
cones, for soccer 227, *228*
contracts, for volunteers 83
count downs 66

diapers, for swimming 149
discs, for soccer 227, *228*
dividing up the space 68, *69*
dojang, the 172, 173, 175
don't bump into me activity 62
dribbling, in soccer *215*, 231–2, *232*

ear protection, for swimming 149
encouragement, tips for 63–4
engagement strategies 74–6
environmental supports 66–71
   assertion 69, *70*
   procedural 67, *67*
   spatial 68–9, *69*
   temporal 66
equipment
   for biking 99–102, *100*, 103–4, *103*
   for martial arts 172
   for skating 124–7, *125*
   for soccer 221–2, *223*
   for swimming 148–50, *149*, 151
   for tennis 194–5
etiquette
   for martial arts 173, 183, *183*
   while skating 128
evaluation, of volunteers 88
extracurricular programs 23–4

failure, dealing with 35
falling
   while biking 113
   while skating 44
family activities 37
feedback, verbal 73
figure eights, while biking 117
first aid 228
first, then, indications 66
fists, making, while doing martial arts 179, *180*
floating, while swimming 158, *159*, *160*
flutter boards, for swimming 150
follow the leader activity 62, 229
football *see* soccer
forward movement, while skating 132–3, *134*
friendships, developing 10
fun, of sports 22

game plans, for soccer 226, *226*
gliding
   while biking 114–15
   while skating 134–5, *135*
   while swimming 160
gloves, for skating 127
goggles, for swimming 149, *149*
gravity, centre of 58
group activities, attitude of children with ASD
   toward 24, 34–5

headgear
   for biking 102, *103*, 104
   for skating 127
   for swimming 150

helmets
  for biking 102, *103*, 104
  for skating 127
hills, while biking 117
hopping, while skating 137–8, *138*

I CAN Play Soccer program 212–16, *215–16*
ice, getting up after falling on 44
ice skating *see* skating
independence
  goals 25
  opportunities for 26
  supports for encouraging 69, *70*
individual activities, attitude of children with ASD
    toward 24
indoor soccer 222
information strategies, for volunteers 78–9
International Ice Hockey Federation 121

joonbi 176, 184, *184*
jumping, while skating 137–8, *138*

kicking
  in soccer *216*, 232–3, *233*
  while doing martial arts 185, *185*
  while swimming 161

learning, benefits of sports for 21–2
learning and development considerations 52–3
learning principles 54–64
  body movement 55–6
  general 54
  influences 56
  new skills 56–63
    balance 57–61, *58*
    visual skill 62, *62*
  tips for encouragement 63–4
learning supports 65–77
  environmental 66–71
    assertion 69, *70*
    procedural 67, *67*, 68
    spatial 68–9, *69*
    temporal 66
  one-to-one 71–4
    modelling 72–4
  strategies to encourage engagement and
      motivation 74–6
    creating structure 74–5
    themes 75
    token systems 76
  teaching and learning 65–6
  visual cues 70–1
lessons
  biking *96*
  skating *124*

soccer *215–16*, *218*
  structure and routines 81–2
  swimming *144*
  tennis *191*
lifejackets 150
likes, children's 30/33, 36
London Football Association 211
loneliness 10, 11
longevity 20

marginalization 10
martial arts 164–87, *165*
  advanced taekwondo skills 186
  balance and weight transfer 61
  basic taekwondo skills 176–85, *177*
    being still 177
    bowing 183, *183*
    deep breathing 178–9, *178*
    horse riding stance 182, *182*
    kicking 185, *185*
    making fists 179, *180*
    ready stance (joonbi) 184, *184*
    training stance 181, *181*
  benefits 164, 166, 168
  definition 165
  first time at the dojang
    arrival 175
    breathing 174
    checking out the studio 173
    checklist 176
    clothing 174
    etiquette 173
    taekwondo terms 174, *175*
  personal story 169–70
  preparation 170–2
    equipment 172
    selecting a program 170–2
  program example 166–8
  success strategies 172
  taekwondo 164–6
mittens, for skating 127
mobile schedules 71
modelling, and one-to-one support 72–4
motivation strategies 74–6
  for tennis 196
  for volunteers 78–9, 86
motor problems 33–4
motor skills 54–64
  fundamental 57
  general learning principles 54
  influences 56
  learning new 56–62
    balance 57–61, *58*
    visual skill 61–2, *62*
  learning to move the body 55–6

name tags 67
nets, for soccer 227
noodles, for swimming 150

obesity, increased risk of 10
one-to-one support 71–4

padding, for biking 102
participation in sports, implications of lack of for kids with ASD 24–5
passing
  in soccer 234–5
  while biking 118
passion, for the sport and for teaching 44–5
pedalling bikes 104–5, 115–16, 117
personal flotation devices (PFDs) 150
personal stories
  about biking 97–8
  about martial arts 169–70
  about skating 126, 131
  about soccer 219–20
  about swimming 146–7
  about tennis 192–3
physical activity
  later in life 22
  recommended level 20
physical guidance 74
  for biking 114
  for skating 130–1, 130, 133
  for swimming 157, 161
physical literacy 20–1
physical traits 36–7
poomsae, the 168, 176, 186
priming story, for soccer 225
procedural supports 67, 67
progress, monitoring 42, 43
pros, tennis 199
protective gear, for biking 102–3, 103

racquets, tennis
  choosing 195
  using 198, 201, 202
  see also strokes: in tennis
rash guards 148
recognition, of volunteers 88
recreation, development of skills for 25
resources, organizations supporting physical activities 27
rule scripts 67, 68
rules
  of the road 118
  of soccer 237

schedules 66, 67, 67, 71
school, activity patterns for children with ASD 23
screening, of volunteers 86
scrimage 217, 236
sensory processing issues 28–9, 31–2
sensory stories 29
shin guards, for soccer 221
shoes, for soccer 221
shooting, in soccer 235–6
shoulder checks, while biking 117
skates, choosing 125
skating 120–40
  advanced skills 139
  balance and weight transfer 61
  basic skills 128–9, 132–9, 133
    gliding 134–5, 135
    hopping 137–8, 138
    moving backward 133
    moving forward 132–3, 134
    skating terms 129
    spinning 138–9, 139
    stopping 136
    twisting and turning 136–7, 136
  benefits 120–1, 121–2
  equipment 124–7
    clothing 127
    helmets 127
    mittens and gloves 127
    skates 125
    visual supports 125
  etiquette 128
  first time on the ice 129–32
    checklist 132
    support 130–1, 130
  personal story 126, 131
  preparation 124–9, 125
  program example 122–4, 124
  reasons for choosing 121
  success strategies 122
  visual support 125
soccer 210–39
  advanced skills 237
  coaches, game plan 226, 226
  first time on the field 227–8, 228
    balls 227
    cones and discs 227, 228
    nets 227
  game time 236–7
    end of game hand circle 238
    field of play 236
    players 236
    rules 237
  history 211
  indoor 222
  personal story 219–20
  preparation 220–5

soccer *cont.*
    checklist 225
    clothing and equipment 221–2, *223*
    playing around with a ball 223
    priming story *225*
    selecting a program 220–1
    soccer terms 224, *224*
    taking a tour 224
  program examples 212–16, 216–19
    typical lessons *215–16, 218*
  reasons for choosing 211
  report card *43*
  success strategies 212
  as a team sport 211–12
  visual support *215*
  warm up and basic skills 228–36, *230*
    ball handling 230, *230*
    dribbling 231–2, *232*
    kicking 232–3, *233*
    passing 234–5
    shooting 235–6
    simple instructional cues 231
    trapping 234
    warm up routines 229, *229*
socialization, goals 25
socks, for soccer 221
spatial supports 68–9, *69*
spinning, while skating 138–9, *139*
stances, for martial arts 181–2, *181, 182*, 184, *184*
steering bikes 104–5
stillness, while doing martial arts 177
stopping, while skating 136
strokes, in tennis *203*, 204–8, *205, 208*
structure, creating 74–5
success strategies
  for biking 99
  for martial arts 172
  for skating 122
  for soccer 212
  for swimming 145, 153, *156*
  for tennis 189
supports, for teaching 40, *41*
swim diapers 149
SwimAbilities program 143–4, *144*
swimmer's wax 149
swimming 141–63
  adult support and physical guidance 157, 160, 161
  advanced skills 161–2
  basic skills 154–61, *155*
    blowing bubbles 154–6, *155, 156*
    floating 158, *159*
    gliding 160
    going underwater 157
    kicking 161
    standing up from a front float 158, *160*

  benefits 141–2
  coping strategies 145
  equipment 147–50
    caps 150
    ear protection 149
    goggles 149, *149*
    swim diapers 149
    swimsuits 148–9
  first time in the pool 151–4
    checklist 154
    getting wet 152
    showering 153
    success strategies 153
    swimming terms 151, *151*
    touring the pool 152
    trying on the equipment 151
    visual support 152
  personal story 146–7
  preparation 144–50
  program example 143–4, *144*
  selecting a program 147
  visual support *145*, 160
swimsuits 148–9

taekwondo *see* martial arts
tandem bikes 111
task analysis 43–4
teaching supports 40, *41*, 65–6
team meetings, for soccer 226
team sport, soccer as a first 211–12
team uniforms, for soccer 222
tee balls, in tennis 203, *203*
temporal supports 66
tennis 188–209
  advanced skills 208–9
  balance and weight transfer 61
  basic skills 199–208, *200–1*
    checklist 200
    contact point 203
    gripping the racquet 201, *202*
    ready position 202
    sideways body position 202–3
    the swing *see* tennis: the swing
    using a tee ball 203, *203*
  benefits 188–9
  personal story 192–3
  preparation 194–9
    ball and racquet experience 198
    checking out the court 198–9
    clothing 194–5
    early ball skills 197–8
    equipment 194–5
    learning skills 194
    meeting the pro 199
    selecting a program 194

supports 195–6
  tennis terms 196–7, *197*
  visual support 196
  watching examples 197
program example 189–91, *191, 192*
success strategies 189
the swing 204–8, *205, 206*
  backhand groundstroke 207
  volley 207–8, *208*
visual support 196
terminology
  biking 105, *105*
  skating 129, *129*
  soccer 224, *224*
  swimming 151, *151*
  taekwondo 174, *175*
  tennis 196–7, *197*
themes, using 75
timers 66
token systems 76
training wheels, for bikes 104
trapping, in soccer 234
turning, while skating 132–3, 136–7
twisting, while skating 136–7

UCLA Adaptive Recreation Programs 190
United States Figure Skating Association 121
United States Tennis Association 190, 195

verbal feedback 73
visual skill 61–2, *62*
visual supports 70–1
  for biking 107, *107*
  for skating *125*
  for soccer *215*
  for swimming *145*, 152, 160
  for tennis 196
vocabulary *see* terminology
volleying, in tennis 207–8, *208*
volunteers 78–89
  checklist about their athlete 84
  contracts 83
  finding 85–6
  information for coaches 86–8
  motivation and information strategies 78–9
  screening 86
  for soccer programs 217
  strategies 80
  supports for 79–81, 79–82

waiting cards 66
warm up routines 62
  for martial arts 175
  for skating *124*
  for soccer 229, *229*
  for tennis 191

water, strategies for introducing 153
water wings 150
weight issues 10
weight transfer
  and balance 59–61
  in tennis 205–6, 207–8
  in water 157, 160

You Can Ride Two program 95–8, *96*
Young Master Club 166–8

zip zones 195, *196*

AUTHOR INDEX

American Red Cross 142

Bachrach, A.W. 142
Baranek, G.T. 53, 121
Bauminger, N. 10
Best, J.F. 142
Boisjoli, J.A. 76
Bondy, A.S. 35
British Taekwondo Control Board 165
Burtton D. 22

Canadian Sport for Life 20–1, 57
Caterino, L. 165
Centers for Disease Control and Prevention 10
Curtin, C. 10

Dalrymple, N.J. 66
Dettmer, S. 66

Etnier, J.L. 19, 21
Evans, R. 70

Ferrer-Caja, E. 22
Finkenberg, M. 165
Frey, C. 23, 25
Frost, L.A, 35
Fuller, J. 165

Gillmeister, H. 188
Grandin, T. 28
Green, F. 25

Hamilton, A. 142
Haskell, W.L. 20
Hemmeter, M.L. 142
Hilton, C.L. 33, 34
Hobbs, K.E. 22

Janzen, J.E. 80
Jasmin, E. 127
Jones, J.G. 142

Kasari, C. 10
Kohl, H.W. 22
Kulhavy, R. 165
Kurian, M. 165
Kurtz, L.A. 56

Lalas, A. 211
Law, M. 19
Lee, I.M. 20
Lee, T.D. 55
Lewis, M. 211

McDuffie, A. 80
Marr, D. 29
Martens, R. 22
Matson, J.L. 76
Ministry of Industry 85

Paffenbarger, R.S. 20
Pan, C. 33
Pan, C.-Y. 23, 25, 142

Ray, M. 25
Rogers, L. 142
Rosser, D.D. 23

Schleien, S. 25
Schmidt, R.P. 55
Sibley, B.A. 19, 21
Skard, O. 22
Stone, W.L. 33

Tissot, C. 70
Tomporowski, P.D. 19, 21
Torbert, M. 56, 58, 61
Trost, S.G. 20

Twemlow, S.W. 165

US Department of Health 19
US Department of Health and Human Services 20
US Soccer Federation 211

Vaglum, P. 22

Weiss, M.R, 22
Wetherby, A.M. 35
Wolery, M. 142

Yilmaz, I. 142
Yoder, P. 80